GST

and Its

AFTERMATH

GST
and Its
AFTERMATH

Is Consumer Really the King?

Govind Bhattacharjee
Debasis Bhattacharya

Los Angeles | London | New Delhi
Singapore | Washington DC | Melbourne

First published in 2018 by

SAGE Publications India Pvt Ltd
B1/I-1 Mohan Cooperative Industrial Area
Mathura Road, New Delhi 110 044, India
www.sagepub.in

SAGE Publications Inc
2455 Teller Road
Thousand Oaks, California 91320, USA

SAGE Publications Ltd
1 Oliver's Yard, 55 City Road
London EC1Y 1SP, United Kingdom

SAGE Publications Asia-Pacific Pte Ltd
3 Church Street
#10-04 Samsung Hub
Singapore 049483

Published by Vivek Mehra for SAGE Publications India Pvt Ltd, typeset in 11/14 pt Cambria by Zaza Eunice, Hosur, Tamil Nadu, India and printed at Sai Print-o-Pack, New Delhi.

Library of Congress Cataloging-in-Publication Data Available

ISBN: 978-93-528-0647-8 (PB)

SAGE Team: Rajesh Dey, Sandhya Gola, Syeda Aina Rahat Ali and Ritu Chopra

Content

List of Illustrations

Tables

Figures

Boxes

List of Abbreviations

AA	advance authorisation
AAR	Advance Ruling Authority
AAAR	Appellate Authority for Advance Ruling
ACCC	Australian Competition and Consumer Commission
API	application programme interface
ASSOCHAM	Associated Chambers of Commerce and Industry of India
BJD	Biju Janata Dal
BMC	Brihanmumbai Municipal Corporation
BSP	Bahujan Samaj Party
BT	business tax
B2B	business-to-business
B2C	business-to-consumer
CAD	current account deficit
CAG	Comptroller and Auditor General
CBEC	Central Board of Excise and Customs
CED	Central Excise Duty
CENVAT	central VAT
CGST	central GST
CII	Confederation of Indian Industry
CPI	consumer price index
CRA	Canada Revenue Agency
CSO	Central Statistical Organisation
CST	Central Sales Tax
CT	consumption tax
C2C	consumer-to-consumer
DMK	Dravida Munnetra Kazhagam

EC	Empowered Committee of State Finance Ministers
EMI	equated monthly instalment
EOU	export oriented unit
EPCG	export promotion capital goods
ERP	enterprise resource planning
EU	European Union
FDI	foreign direct investment
FIEO	Federation of Indian Export Organisations
FIIs	foreign institutional investments
FMCG	fast-moving consumer goods
FRBMA	Fiscal Responsibility and Budget Management Act
FST	Federal Sales Tax
FTP	Foreign Trade Policy
GDP	gross domestic product
GFCE	government final consumption expenditure
GFCG	gross fixed capital formation
GSPs	GST Suvidha Providers
GST	Goods and Services Tax
GSTIN	GST Identification Number
GSTN	GST Network
GVA	gross value added
G2B	government-to-business
HSD	high-speed diesel
HSN	Harmonised System of Nomenclature
HST	Harmonized Sales Tax
IGST	inter-state GST
IIP	Index of Industrial Production
JD(S)	Janata Dal (Secular)
JD(U)	Janata Dal (United)
MASH sector	municipalities, academic institutions (including universities), schools and hospitals
MODVAT	modified VAT

MRP	maximum retail price
MRTP Act	Monopolies and Restrictive Trade Practices Act
MSMEs	micro, small and medium enterprises
MST	Manufacturers' Sales Tax
NCP	Nationalist Congress Party
NELP	New Exploration and Licensing Policy
NPAs	non-performing assets
NPISHs	non-profit institutions serving households
PANs	permanent account numbers
PCP	Progressive Conservative Party
PFCE	private final consumption expenditure
PSBs	public sector banks
PSTs	provincial sales taxes
PSUs	public sector undertakings
QST	Québec Sales Tax
RAI	Retailers Association of India
RBI	Reserve Bank of India
RJD	Rashtriya Janata Dal
RST	regional sales tax
RTO	Regional Transport Office
SAC	Services Accounting Code
SAD	special additional duty
SGST	state GST
SKU	stock keeping unit
SMEs	small and medium enterprises
SP	Samajwadi Party
TICPE	Taxe Intérieure de Consommation sur les Produits Énergétiques
TRS	Telangana Rashtra Samithi
TVA	*Taxe sur la Valeur Ajoutée*
UTGST	Union Territory Goods and Services Tax
UTs	union territories
VAT	value-added tax

MRP	maximum retail price
MRTP Act	Monopolies and Restrictive Trade Practices Act
MSMEs	micro, small and medium enterprises
MST	Manufacturers' Sales Tax
NCP	Nationalist Congress Party
NELP	New Exploration and Licensing Policy
NPAs	non-performing assets
NPISHs	non-profit institutions serving households
PANs	permanent account numbers
PCP	Progressive Conservative Party
PFCE	private final consumption expenditure
PSBs	public sector banks
PSTs	provincial sales taxes
PSUs	public sector undertakings
QST	Québec Sales Tax
RAI	Retailers Association of India
RBI	Reserve Bank of India
RJD	Rashtriya Janata Dal
RST	regional sales tax
RTO	Regional Transport Office
SAC	Services Accounting Code
SAD	special additional duty
SGST	state GST
SKU	stock keeping unit
SMEs	small and medium enterprises
SP	Samajwadi Party
TICPE	Taxe Intérieure de Consommation sur les Produits Énergétiques
TRS	Telangana Rashtra Samithi
TVA	*Taxe sur la Valeur Ajoutée*
UTGST	Union Territory Goods and Services Tax
UTs	union territories
VAT	value-added tax

Preface

Goods and Services Tax (GST) has divided the intelligentsia of the country into two distinct warring camps: one holding that it will usher in unprecedented prosperity for the country within the foreseeable future and the other believing in just the opposite—that it will take the country to the brink of a grim economic disaster from which recovery will be difficult. These extreme opinions are often coloured by the political philosophies of the opposing camps, and truth, as always, probably lies somewhere in between. But even its most outspoken detractors do not deny that it has been an important milestone in the history of our economic reforms. The contentious arguments based on conflicting economic rationales, and the enormous volumes of relevant and irrelevant statistics flaunted by the supporters and opponents of the tax reform have left the common man utterly confounded. Reams of newsprints and hundreds of hours of TV time consumed by the subject have brought little clarity and enlightenment to the common man about the intended benefits and pitfalls of GST and about how to handle the difficult transition phase it is going through. This is simply because a reform of such monumental complexity has never before been attempted in our country, and there is no precedence to be guided by, nor many lessons from our history of tax reforms to learn from and use in relation to a multifaceted, disruptive and transformational reform such as the GST. The only guidance available is from the other countries which have already switched over to a similar regime, but few, if any, have as complex a federal set-up as ours, given the size and population of our country, with so much of diversity, complexity and asymmetry between its constituent parts. Just to understand the basics of this reform would be a daunting task to most, let alone trying to explain it to others.

It was, therefore, natural that when we were requested to explore this uncharted arena and attempt to demystify the many myths surrounding GST for the common man, given that there was no book available from which the common taxpayer and consumer can derive some clarity and understanding about the subject, it was with a great deal of trepidation and hesitation that we undertook the task. There was practically nothing to guide us except the compendia of the relevant statutes, which were the only resources available, besides media reports. It was a great challenge, but I must confess that at the end of it, we have been much enriched in our own understanding of the subject and the issues at stake, and it has all throughout been an extremely meaningful learning experience for us. If this book succeeds in making these issues a little clearer to the layman for whom this book is written, that will be our highest reward.

The common man, who can be either a consumer or a taxpayer, has always been at our focal point in this entire endeavour, and the book is primarily written for him. While never losing sight of our focus, we have nevertheless been always mindful of the fact that a book on a difficult subject like this cannot be attempted without the academic rigour that it demands, and we have tried not to dilute it. By and large, we have tried to avoid technical jargon and difficult economic concepts; where we could not, the terms and concepts have been explained in simple language for the lay reader. This book is divided into six chapters of which the first four have been contributed by me and the last two by my co-author, Dr Debasis Bhattacharya.

Chapter 1, 'Another Freedom at Midnight', deals with the launching of GST after three decades of strenuous efforts undertaken by different governments and the euphoria as well as the apprehensions surrounding the event. The complexity of the erstwhile indirect tax regime GST is supposed to replace has also been briefly addressed in this chapter.

Chapter 2, 'At the End of a Long Journey', describes the difficult journey spread over 3 decades and negotiated by 9 prime ministers and 12 finance ministers of the country that has finally culminated in launching the landmark reform on 1 July 2017 by working out a rare consensus in our political democracy. The chapter narrates the political and constitutional hurdles that had to be overcome in the way, and discusses the dynamics of the new tax architecture.

Chapter 3, 'Insights from the Travails of Other Pioneers', deals with the experiences of some of the other countries with their GSTs—Canada, European Union, Australia, Malaysia and also China. Federal countries are more relevant to our situation; hence, we have extensively dealt with the experience of Canada whose dual model of federal and provincial GST resembles our own GST system in many ways. Each of these countries had faced serious problems while implementing their own GSTs and had negotiated a difficult transition phase from which there is much to learn. Many of the pitfalls experienced by them are now being faced by us in much the same manner. GST everywhere has followed more or less the same track and run the same course, causing disruptions and turbulence in the initial phases before the system attained its equilibrium. Everywhere, growth declined and inflation soared in the immediate aftermath of the launch of GST, and everywhere growth bounced back and inflation came under control after the initial turbulence was over. If the situation is managed well, there is no reason why our experiences should be any different.

In Chapter 4, 'Overcoming Hurdles and Challenges', we have discussed some of the difficulties and challenges in implementing the complex reform and how it is impacting some of the vital sectors of our economy, especially the informal sector with vast numbers of micro, small and medium entities which operate without adequate infrastructure and capacity to handle the technology-driven new tax system, and the exporters who are in a sort of logjam due to the backbone of the new tax architecture—the GST Network—not yet being able to function with optimum efficiency. The cost of compliance is an issue yet to be addressed effectively, and we have described the initiatives the government has taken so far to make life a little easier for the multitudes of small players who are the primary drivers of our economic ecosystem.

Written by Dr Bhattacharya, Chapter 5, 'Goodbye to Tax Terrorism', discusses the prospects of GST for curbing tax terrorism and the use of black money. Replacement of a regressive and distortionary indirect tax structure with multiple taxes levied at multiple points is in itself heart-warming for the taxpayers due to the relief it is supposed to bring from the army of tax inspectors and a plethora of tax returns they had to deal with in the earlier regime. The extent to which GST can eliminate the interface with these inspectors will determine the success of the new tax regime. Once technology drives transactions in increasing numbers into the formal network, the use of black money will tend to be limited. Success on both these fronts will of course depend on the implementation management.

The last chapter of this book, Chapter 6, 'Voice of the People', takes the book to its climax, because here we have dealt directly with the stakeholders in real life. Dr Bhattacharya has painstakingly interviewed the stakeholders from different walks of life to assess the impact of the new tax regime on their activities and budgets—from the local *kirana* (grocery) stores to trades and businesses that impact the life of every citizen, as well as consumers and tax administrators. He has elicited their detailed responses through extended personal interviews over the last two months to find out what problems GST has created for each and what prospects it has opened up for the common man, who is the ultimate focus of this book. This experience was highly insightful and revealing for us.

It is to be understood that at this stage, GST is an evolving process, and the law and procedures have already been modified substantially, bringing the tax rates on many items much lower than originally envisaged and making the system of compliance much simpler. We have taken into account some of the important decisions taken at the 23rd meeting of the GST Council, recently held in November 2017, and updated the book accordingly. As and when changes are made, our conclusions would also stand modified to that extent. But, as of now, GST is far from what it was envisaged to be: a simple, single-rate, unified tax covering all commodities in the country and making India a truly unfragmented common market. It is certainly not a magic pill for all our economic malaises, and stabilising it will still take a long time before it starts delivering its intended benefits, that is, if the transition is managed well. No country on earth has ever attempted such a complex reform of this scale and magnitude, and it takes a lot of courage and boldness to embark upon such a reform fraught with so much of risk, economic as well as political.

One common criticism which has been hurled at GST too often is that it has been launched rather hastily, without adequate preparation and without giving its design long enough time to prevent the problems that we are now facing. In our fractious political climate, it has already taken us three decades to arrive at the political consensus necessary to launch this reform that has replaced multiple taxes and cesses by a single tax covering both the Centre and the states—something that was long overdue and carries the promise of transforming our economic landscape by setting the creative potential of our entrepreneurs and businesses free from structural constraints. No tax system could claim to be flawless, and GST indeed has its own drawbacks and shortcomings. But instead of waiting an eternity to design and implement a perfect system, it was much more pragmatic to start with a less than perfect one and then go along correcting the glitches as and when they surface.

Sure enough, there will be problems and disruptions galore. But the important thing is to make a beginning when we have in sight our goals and the sincerity of purpose. We now need to manage the change with the same sense of purpose, with a resolute determination and faith in our hearts that 'we shall overcome'. To this end, we dedicate this book to all the citizens and taxpayers of our country—especially to the nameless millions of small traders and entrepreneurs on whose growth depends the growth of the country and the prosperity of our future generations.

New Delhi   **Govind Bhattacharjee**
18 December 2017

Acknowledgements

Many friends and colleagues have extended their help in writing this book which was a daunting challenge for us. Without their constant support and encouragement, we could not have completed this work so soon. First and foremost, our thanks are due to the publishers, without whose determined urging and constant encouragement, we would not have undertaken such a difficult task in the first place. Ms Srijan Bhan, a brilliant undergraduate student of the Lady Sriram College, New Delhi, had very kindly offered her assistance to help us with the background research. She had meticulously collected scores of articles on the subject from various journals and newspapers, national as well as international, through hours of painstaking library work and forwarded these to us. These rich resources provided by her were of invaluable help throughout, and we gratefully acknowledge her contribution for this book. Her unfailing sincerity and keenness to learn earned our highest appreciation, and we take this opportunity to wish her all the best for her future.

We take this opportunity to thank Mr Shashank Priya, Joint Secretary, GST Council, Government of India, for graciously agreeing to clarify some of the most vexing issues regarding GST. The learned colleagues of Dr Govind Bhattacharjee, Mr P. K. Mishra, and Mr Mukesh P. Singh, with whom we have had many pleasant hours of fruitful discussions on many of the issues that have featured in this book, deserve our thanks and gratitude; these discussions have cleared many of our doubts and helped crystallise our thoughts on the subject.

Ms Amrita K. Bhattacharya, a PhD student at Jadavpur University, Kolkata, provided some useful research articles on the subject. Mr Ravinder Kumar and Mr Mahender Singh from the Secretariat of Dr Govind Bhattacharjee rendered invaluable help in systematically collecting all relevant reports on the subject over an extended period of the last two years, ever since GST had started occupying media space. They collected and organised hundreds of these reports and without their help, we could never have completed this work. We owe all of them many thanks for their efforts.

Dr Debasis Bhattacharya personally thanks all the traders and members of business communities he had interviewed for sparing their valuable time even in the midst of a very busy festive season to relate their experiences with GST, and also all the consumers he had spoken to for evaluating the impact of GST upon their lives. He thanks his mother, Mrs Bijaya Bhattacharyya, who had been a constant source of inspiration and encouragement for him throughout the work. Dr Govind Bhattacharjee thanks his wife, Dr Rakhee Bhattacharjee, Associate Professor at Jawaharlal Nehru University, New Delhi, who has offered many useful pieces of advice from time to time, which have added value to the book.

To all of them and to many others who have not been named, we owe our deepest gratitude.

Chapter One

Another Freedom at Midnight

The Midnight Dawn

Midnight of 1 July 2017 was a landmark moment—a moment of monumental significance in the economic and political history of independent India. Although there cannot be any comparison between events which are vastly different in tenor and significance, somehow this moment was a reminder of another time in history when a newborn nation had made its tryst with destiny after making a singular transition from servitude to liberation, waking to light and freedom at the stroke of the midnight hour of 15 August 1947. That was when we had earned our political freedom from the oppressive and brutish rule of the British Raj after a long and hard struggle, shaking off the yoke of nearly two centuries of servitude. It also brought the memory of another time, when pushed to the wall by an equally oppressive License–Permit Raj regime, we had decided to dismantle, once and for all, a command and control structure that was stifling our economy and stymieing the growth of a youthful nation. That was on 24 July 1991 when the finance minister of the Narasimha Rao government, Dr Manmohan Singh, had risen to deliver his maiden Budget speech, selling the dream to usher India into the twenty-first century by unleashing the creative energy and entrepreneurship of a nation that was for long held captive by a corrupt and short-sighted ruling political class, in an unholy nexus with an equally corrupt, inefficient and unimaginative bureaucracy. 'For the creation of wealth, we must encourage accumulation of capital', Dr Singh asserted and went on to place his faith in the market forces rather than the dated Nehruvian ideas of economic growth. Those ideas were derived from a flawed Soviet-type centralised planning model in which the public sector was supposed to be the primary driver of industrialisation in the country and to dominate the 'commanding heights' of the economy. In the pursuit of ushering in a 'socialistic pattern of society', the private sector was looked at with suspicion and its growth stifled by putting it under all kinds of controls and restrictions, and by limiting its access only to a few sectors of the economy, while the core sectors were reserved for the public sector only. The unrelenting experimentation with socialistic economic ideas during the first four decades of our existence as an independent sovereign nation had miserably failed to create the opportunities needed for a young nation to grow. Poverty and lack of economic opportunities seemed to be our only inevitable destiny. Recognising the formidable difficulties that lay ahead on the long and arduous journey to economic freedom, and echoing the words of Victor Hugo that 'No power on earth can stop an idea whose time has come', Dr Singh had declared emphatically, 'The emergence of India as a major economic power in the world happens to be one such idea. Let the whole world hear it loud and clear. India is now wide awake. We shall prevail. We shall overcome'. In that moment began our journey to economic freedom, and this journey has since pulled nearly a quarter of a billion people out of poverty. The journey we had embarked upon then has made us one of the fastest growing emerging economies in the world, helping us to shed finally the stale image of the 'Sick Man of Asia'.

1 July 2017 should now mark the beginning of our freedom from tax and inspector raj, the incredibly complex, obnoxious and cascading system of taxation with grossly unfair entry barriers that has been holding our industry and the economy from realising their full potential. Launching a measure that promises to unify India into one nation, one market and one tax system; help in curtailing the dominance of black money; and free the common people from the scourge of tax terrorism, Prime Minister Narendra Modi had invoked the country's first home minister, 'The GST is an economic integration of India just like what Sardar Vallabhbhai Patel had done decades back to integrate the country'. It was a measure indeed for the integration and simplification of the tax regime, a daring and bold step not many countries have shown the courage to embrace so far. At a glittering ceremony in the packed Central Hall of Parliament, where 70 years ago Nehru had given his 'Tryst of Destiny' speech, at the stroke of midnight hour, President Pranab Mukherjee and Prime Minister Narendra Modi pressed the button to officially launch the Goods and Services Tax (GST). Among the host of dignitaries on the dais were former vice-president Hamid Ansari, Finance Minister Arun Jaitley, Speaker Sumitra Mahajan and former prime minister, H. D. Deve Gowda, while ministers and bureaucrats and people from different walks of life representing the entire microcosm of the Indian society—business, trade, industry, media and celebrities—constituted the audience in the Hall. However, the opposition, fractious and divided as they are, could not forget their differences and came together with the government on the same platform even on such a historic occasion. While the Janata Dal (United) (JD[U]), the Nationalist Congress Party (NCP), the Biju Janata Dal (BJD), the Samajwadi Party (SP) and Janata Dal (Secular) (JD[S]) participated in the midnight event, the Congress party, which had

initiated the proposal for GST years ago, boycotted the occasion along with Trinamool Congress, the Left and some other parties, which some sections of the media termed as 'midnight churlishness'. The last midnight event when the Parliament was lit up so brightly was in 1997, on the occasion of the golden jubilee of our Independence. But the present occasion indeed marked a new kind of independence.

Addressing the gathering just before the launch of the unified tax system, the president, who as the finance minister under UPA II had introduced the Constitution (One Hundred and Fifteenth Amendment) Bill in 2011 that had brought GST within the realms of a certainty, said that the roll-out of the indirect tax regime was 'a tribute to the maturity and wisdom of India's democracy'. He called GST a 'disruptive change', a consensus between the Centre and states, and an effort 'from persons across the political spectrum who set aside narrow partisan considerations and put the nation's interests first'. A change is disruptive only when it creates a massive shift in the way a system functioned. It sometimes ushers in what the Harvard economist Joseph Schumpeter had called 'creative destruction'—a process of renewal in society and economy in which the old order changes, yielding place to the new, in the process destroying old ways, replacing old methods and outdated technologies with new ones, making existing technologies, methods and procedures obsolete, and turning winners in the old system losers in the new. Fear of creative destruction, as Daron Acemoglu and James Robinson had argued in their insightful book *Why Nations Fail*, is often at the root of opposition to building inclusive political and economic institutions and, hence, precluding higher economic growth of societies that only such institutions can ensure.

Earlier, the Prime Minister had acknowledged that 'This is not the achievement of any one political party or any one government. This is the collective legacy of all, a result of the collective efforts of all'. Reiterating that 'GST is a transparent and fair system that prevents black money and corruption and promotes new governance culture', he compared the new indirect tax regime as a shining example of cooperative federalism: 'India is an example of cooperative federalism. It is the result of long and continuous thought process'.

A long and continuous process indeed it has been to reform our archaic, antiquated tax system. It was designed to extract from all businesses as much as it could, with a plethora of taxes a producer, supplier or distributor of goods and services had to negotiate and pay, and the preposterous mazes of tax returns one had to prepare and file. At every stage in the process, one had to encounter an abundance of tax officials who will descend uninvited upon any industry or business establishment, and they needed to be propitiated, in cash or kind, not to speak of the incessant harassment and humiliation they had to face from these crooked officials. Our multi-layered, multi-point, multi-tax system was one among the most complex in the world and was a legacy from the exploitative and extractive colonial rule. The taxes on a commodity or service were compounded at every stage, hiking up prices of the product and creating channels of corruption and leakage at every stage. Under the tyranny of the taxmen, rent-seeking flourished, cost of business increased manifolds, and trade and commerce became the hapless victim. The present GST, in the form it has been introduced, is still a far cry from the 'Good and Simple Tax' the Prime Minister wishes it to be, but compared to the situation half a century ago, it must look like a revolutionary progress. As Finance Minister Arun Jaitley had remarked, the implementation of this landmark and unified tax should be seen as the beginning of a new journey that will expand the country's economic horizon. It indeed has the potential to end the harassment of taxpayers, but what kind of governance culture it will promote remains to be seen, as much as its efficacy in curbing black money and corruption.

It is still far from perfect, but instead of spending an eternity in devising and perfecting a system before introducing it, it was certainly much more pragmatic to have made a beginning, which itself was a paradigm shift, with an imperfect system and then go on correcting the glitches its implementation will throw up from time to time—rectifying the mistakes as and when they occur and removing the imperfections as we move along in slow, gradual but sure steps. A highly fragmented and divided system cannot be perfected and unified at one go, especially in a complex country like India where multiple disruptive forces exert and assert their pulls and pressures in different directions, making it impossible to establish any sustained equilibrium at any given point of time. Even a virulent critic of the current regime like the previous Finance Minister Mr P. Chidambaram, who earlier had attempted to bring in a GST, had to concede,

> Many of the flaws in the design were the result of forced political compromise. It seems to me too much has been compromised and for reasons that are not apparent. Anyway, we have a baby. It is not a bonny baby, it has some birth defects, it must be carefully nurtured, but it is our baby and let me therefore welcome the new baby.[1]

The baby is born with the promise to lower the tax burden by eliminating the cascading effects of a plethora of central and state taxes, cesses and surcharges—and to facilitate free movement of goods across the borders of our 29 states. If the promises are fulfilled, then perhaps, 'From Ganganagar to Itanagar, from Leh to Lakshadweep, the dream of one nation, one tax will be fulfilled', as the Prime Minister has hoped. Even if it is fulfilled partially, still it would be a big achievement.

---

[1] P. Chidambaram, 'GST Rollout: Get Set for Turbulence', *Indian Express*, 2 September 2017.

Reactions of the stakeholders to the roll-out of this unique tax have been mixed. Some welcomed it enthusiastically, some were highly sceptical, while some reacted with guarded caution. Excitement, exhilaration and nervousness played out in equal measures among different stakeholders. The credit-rating agency Moody's thinks that the implementation of GST will be positive for India's rating as it will lead to higher GDP[2] growth and increased tax revenues. Its Vice-President William Foster said, 'Over the medium term, we expect that the GST will contribute to productivity gains and higher GDP growth by improving the ease of doing business, unifying the national market and enhancing India's attractiveness as a foreign investment destination'. He hoped that GST will support higher government revenue generation through improved tax compliance and administration, both of which will be positive for India's credit profile, which is constrained by a relatively low revenue base. Moody's has a 'Baa3' rating on India with a positive outlook.

The Confederation of Indian Industry (CII) also exuded hope: 'We have emerged … into a new era of economic reform with the introduction of the game-changing GST. This will stand as an exemplar of collaborative reform for the world on an unprecedented scale', its president said and hoped that GST would impart major competitiveness to Indian industry, incentivise exports, give tremendous confidence to industry and contribute to the ease of doing business. The Associated Chambers of Commerce and Industry of India (ASSOCHAM), which is the oldest body with more than 400 industry chambers and trade associations and is referred to as the 'Chamber of Chambers'

---

[2] Gross domestic product (GDP) is the value of all goods and services produced in a country during a period, usually a year. It can also be expressed in terms of gross value added (GVA) to the economy as GDP = GVA + taxes on products – subsidies on products.

with more than 4.5 lakh[3] corporate members, said that with retail prices growing by the slowest pace in the last four years, the timing for GST was perfect from the inflation point of view. It said,

> In the backdrop of subdued consumer demand, there is no reason for the industry not to pass on any benefit accruing from the GST. The top priority for the industry today is to step up its capacity utilisation by increasing production, helped by consumer demand.

Media reacted with caution, but not without enthusiasm. 'There was something undeniably momentous about the Joint Session of Parliament that formally began the process of bringing together the country's 2 trillion dollar economy and 1.3 billion consumers into a single market', *The Indian Express* observed.[4] It went on to assert that 'The sheer scale of the GST makes it one of the most complex tax reforms attempted anywhere in the world', even though 'What was launched on Friday midnight may not be the perfect tax regime'. *The Hindu* commented,

> In a landmark reform, India today switches to a new indirect tax system, the Goods and Services Tax….The reform has been years in the making, and having shown the political will to finally pull it off, the Central government must work with the States to chart a road map to simplify the tax regime.[5]

'It took a combined effort by India's political parties to set aside narrow interests in the pursuit of greater common good to bring about this reform', *The Times of India* reminded, 'However, switching over to GST should not be seen as an end in itself. Instead it should be seen as the beginning of a process

---

[3] 1 lakh = 0.1 million; 1 crore = 10 million.
[4] *The Indian Express*, 'In a New Regime', *The Indian Express*, 3 July 2017.
[5] *The Hindu*, 'Midnight Makeover: Adoption of GST', *The Hindu*, 1 July 2017.

of reform to truly unshackle the Indian economy'.[6] In a feel-good rally on the back of GST launch, both the Sensex and Nifty gained 1 per cent each on Monday, 4 July 2017, and ended near their respective all-time highs. The Sensex gained 300 points to close at 31,222.

The BJP predictably lauded the Prime Minister,

> GST will reset the basic rules of taxation. It is an illustration of PM Modi's transformative reforms. Modi is on a transformative agenda, the fruits of which will be borne by this nation in a few years' time. He is setting India's basics right with a futuristic vision.[7]

The Congress, equally predictably, condemned it, 'A reform that holds great potential is being rushed through in a half-baked way with a self-promotional spectacle.... But like demonetisation, GST is being executed by an incompetent and insensitive government without planning, foresight and institutional readiness'.[8]

Different segments of industry reacted differently, depending on what was at stake. Tax consultants and consultant firms rejoiced, as GST is expected to spawn a US$2–3 billion (₹13,000 crore–₹20,000 crore) additional business for the industry comprising software service providers, chartered accountants and consulting firms as the entire industry is undergoing business process reengineering. Deloitte has already recruited 250 professionals for its indirect tax team, PricewaterhouseCoopers has also expanded their pool of chartered accountants and system executives by 200–250, while ClearTax has hired as many as 400 people to deal with the additional workload. SAP

---

[6] *The Times of India*, 'Force Multiplier: GST Is Just the Beginning, Reform to Truly Unshackle the Indian Economy', *The Times of India*, 3 July 2017.

[7] Ram Madhav, 'Like a Bee Gathers Honey', *The Indian Express*, 4 July 2017.

[8] *Hindustan Times*, 'Rahul Gandhi Calls GST Half-baked Reform, Rollout a Tamasha', *Hindustan Times*, 1 July 2017.

has deployed 500–600 people to provide services to clients. But nervousness was palpable among the firms, especially the small and medium enterprises (SMEs). Nearly 90 lakh firms were required to upload every detail of their business transactions onto the technology-based GST Network (GSTN) that sits at the heart of the complex GST architecture (explained later).

From the largest firms to the smallest mobile retail sellers, everyone has been getting ready for the new tax law. Their business costs have increased for complying with the requirements of the new law, and the requirement of filing of monthly returns has made many accountants raise their fees. But consumers were in for a bonanza; pre-GST sale of the e-tailers, supermarkets and malls in cities peaked as the launch was getting nearer with huge discounts offered on the products, resembling a mini-Diwali. Manufacturers and traders were busy clearing their stocks, being uncertain how things would shape up post GST. They were playing on the side of caution. But small traders were especially terrified, and they were not equipped, financially or technologically, to install and operate computers or hire full-time accountants for their small establishments to prepare for the transition to the new indirect tax regime. Some textile workers and small traders went on sporadic strikes.

As is natural with implementation of any new system, especially one based on cutting-edge technology like GST, there were glitches and confusion galore. Several large companies had to virtually shut down their operations while switching to the new regime for updating their software and invoicing systems. Mapping of the so-called HSN[9] Codes (provided by CBEC)

---

[9] Harmonised System of Nomenclature is a six-digit coding system of tariff nomenclature for classification of products used mainly for customs duty purposes. It is an internationally standardised system of names and numbers to classify traded goods between different countries. Central Board of Excise and Customs (CBEC) is the apex body responsible for administration of indirect taxes in the country.

with the items was proving a big technological hurdle. Traders felt that the implementation was done rather hastily, giving them little time to adapt and integrate into the countrywide taxing system of digitised accounts and periodic filing of tax returns. Even those who have registered with the GSTN were apprehensive of the post-implementation glitches. Clarity was also missing about using the GST software. One confused trader sought divine help, saying, 'I'm depending on Lord Hanuman, not government, for guidance'. Another voiced his frustration, 'This new system does nothing but exploit small traders. I have registered because there is no other choice. I might still change career if things don't work out'.[10]

Days after the launch of the new tax regime, problems had not subsided still. A team of 10 central government officers stationed at the GST Feedback and Action Room of the Finance Ministry was putting in 14 hours a day, right from 8 in the morning, to monitor real-time feedback on the transition from across the country. Doubts relating to registration, rates, returns, refunds, migration etc. were attempted to be clarified through full-page FAQs inserted in all newspapers on a daily basis by the CBEC. The turbulence was expected to last for yet some time, despite GST Seva Kendras claimed to have been set up by the CBEC in every range under every commissionerate throughout the country, where field-level officers—inspectors and superintendents—were ready to help the taxpayers, equipped with state-of-the-art computers. Presumably, traders who hoarded black money were scared and certainly resentful of a tax system that made them a part of a tax net, as tax evasion would become difficult with transactions getting digitised and, hence, capable of being tracked.

---

[10] *The Times of India*, 'For These Traders, GST Still a Riddle', *The Times of India*, 1 July 2017.

But on the ground, the check posts erected earlier by the states have disappeared along with the bribe-happy tax officials and cops. These check posts, which used to clog traffic for hours, delaying shipment of goods and causing avoidable harassment to the truck drivers, have already been dispensed by many states. Some, like Karnataka, will stop trucks only to verify if the goods are as declared on the GSTN web portal. This system will continue until its replacement in the form of electronic or e-way bills takes off. The lathi-wielding inspectors and officials from the commercial tax department, conspicuously seen at the Delhi–Noida border on NH24, who often used to erect barricades and stopped almost every commercial vehicle, were, however, still operating, though on a lesser scale. Apparently, UP, thus, has removed the check posts only on paper. While state commercial tax department's check posts will disappear, local bodies, however, will still need the commercial vehicles to stop for collecting taxes from them, such as the ones erected by the three municipal corporations of Delhi. Brihanmumbai Municipal Corporation (BMC), the only local body in Maharashtra which collects octroi, has volunteered to do away with check posts. Some states had done it even before GST was introduced such as Haryana, Gujarat, West Bengal, Maharashtra, UP, Odisha, Chhattisgarh and Rajasthan, while Karnataka, Tamil Nadu and Andhra Pradesh have dismantled these check posts after the introduction of GST. All other states and union territories (UTs) are also doing so.

Road transport by trucks accounts for 65 per cent of the freight volume in India. At every state border, a truck transporting goods had to stop—and wait for hours in a queue—in order to pay the entry taxes to the state government; as a result, their movement remained slow and suboptimal. Despite the vast improvements in road infrastructure, entry barriers at state borders—some of which are notorious like the one between Assam and West Bengal—have ensured that the average distance travelled by vehicles remained at the same level for the last few years. The avoidable delay in truck movements is estimated to cost the economy over ₹40,000 crore a year, apart from loss of fuel, as an IIM Calcutta study had estimated. All trucks under the earlier system had to halt at the state borders, even though only 1 per cent was non-compliant as far as documentation requirements were concerned. To clear the logjam, the Centre has suggested a risk-based assessment followed by e-way bills to ensure trucks can move across borders freely. The initiative is to gather momentum as yet, but this is what GST was aiming at, free movement of trade and commerce across the country and transforming India into a single common market, in fulfilling the Constitutional promises. One month after the roll-out of GST, the truck movement has already been reported to have become faster by as much as 30 per cent, now covering about 300 km a day.

The Regime of Complexity Unbounded

Article 301 of the Constitution—the first article of Part XIII of the Constitution dealing with 'Trade, Commerce and Intercourse Within the Territory of India'—indeed promised a common market for the country by providing that trade commerce and intercourse through the territory of India shall be free. It does not promise freedom from the imposition of taxes and duties but only ensures that such imposition does not result in the restriction of trade and commerce. It does not provide freedom from laws but only freedom from those laws that burden, restrict or prevent movements of trade and commerce between and within the states. Numerous Supreme Court judgements[11] have reaffirmed this from time to time, but

---

[11] Jindal Stainless Ltd v. State of Haryana, [2006] AIR SC 2550: [2006] AIR SCW 3396: [2006] 2 All CJ 1216: [2006] 2383 ITR 1: [2006] 7 SCC 241: [2006] 4 SCALE 300: [2006] 3 Supreme 593: [2006] 194 Taxation 525. There are many other cases as well.

they have failed to improve the ground reality. The dream of a uniform market for all India to facilitate seamless movement of goods and services has remained a chimera for the last 70 years. Article 302 deals with the power of the Parliament to impose restrictions on trade, commerce and intercourse in public interest, but neither the Parliament nor any state legislature has the power to enact any law that made one state more preferable to another in respect of trade and commerce by virtue of any entry into the Seventh Schedule, as per Article 303, except in situations of scarcity. Article 304, however, enables a state to impose a tax on inter-state trade—especially on imports from other states—to equalise between the prices of manufactured and imported goods. Thus, the spirit of the Constitution is clear from these Articles—to promote and ensure unrestrained inter-state trade and movement of goods between states.

Reality, as always, was, however, quite different. There were restrictions all the way. Not only that, but there was also a plethora of taxes on each commodity imposed at different stages of their journey from the factory to the market and onwards to the consumer; whenever a tax was imposed on the goods at any stage—during production, distribution or sale—the taxes got compounded, hiking up the final cost of the product. Since at each stage, some taxes had to be paid either to the Centre or to the states, at every subsequent stage, it was only leading to payment of tax on taxes—a cascading effect that was working against all industrial and business growth. There were thus 17 indirect taxes—8 levied by the Centre and 9 by the states—that a commodity was subject to at various stages of their journey to the consumer after production in the factory, affecting manufacturers, wholesalers and retailers equally.

Taxes are levied by the Centre and the states depending on their respective jurisdictions as defined in the Union and the State Lists under the Seventh Schedule to the Constitution of India. For the Centre or the state to levy a tax on any subject, there has to be a corresponding taxing entry in the concerned list. The jurisdictions of the Centre and the states in this respect are non-overlapping, as there is no taxing entry in the Concurrent List. India may be one country under the same political system, but it operates like 29 different economies, with each state imposing its own set of taxes, over and above the taxes imposed by the Centre.

The complexity of the system was indeed mind-boggling. To give a few examples, the central excise was a tax on manufacturing, levied when the manufactured goods were being moved out of the factory and collected by the Centre (the Central Excise department). The value-added tax (VAT) or sales tax was a tax on sale of these products levied and collected by the states. It was paid by the consumers, but the seller had the responsibility to collect and pay the tax to the Department of Sales Tax. On manufacture of certain products, most notably alcohol, the excise duty was imposed by the states and not the Centre. On top of the Union excise duty, there were additional excise duties levied on several products—for example, 'goods of special importance' such as tobacco and sugar, and textile and textile products, besides excise duty on toilet and medicinal preparation containing alcohol—under separate statutes.[12] The Centre levies customs duty to be collected by the Customs department on the import of goods, but over and above the basic customs duty, the Centre could also impose an additional customs duty as well as a special additional duty (SAD). The additional customs duty is also known as the countervailing duty which was imposed to counter the negative impact of export subsidies to protect domestic producers by equalising prices on imported and manufactured goods—this was applicable when imported products enjoyed export subsidies

---

[12] Additional Duties of Excise (Goods of Special Importance) Act, 1957; Additional Duties of Excise (Textiles and Textile Articles) Act, 1978. Some of these duties had already become obsolete.

in countries where they were being produced and thus were cheaper than their domestically produced counterparts. This often serves as a measure to prevent dumping of products by exporters. In case of inter-state trade, when any good entered a state, an entry tax was to be paid by the importer of the good to his state; even within the state, when goods moved into another municipality, another entry tax called 'octroi' was to be paid to the municipality. Ordinary human mind would certainly falter while attempting to make any sense of this incredible multiplicity and complexity of the archaic Indian tax system inherited from the British.

On top of the taxes were the cesses and surcharges; in fact, they have been proliferating at a regular rate. Under article 271, Centre alone has the power to impose any surcharge on any of the taxes levied by it, and while the proceeds from all other Union taxes are sharable with the states, as recommended by the Finance Commissions, surcharges were not, and Centre could keep the entire proceeds from surcharges for its own purposes. Same with cess, which is a tax for a specific purpose and the proceeds of which should be retained and used exclusively for that purpose, which is often not the case. Cess and surcharge which are levied as a small percentage of some taxes end up increasing the effective rates of those taxes, for example, the 0.5 per cent Krishi Kalyan Cess levied with effect from June 2016 on all taxable services raised its effective rate from 14.5 per cent to 15 per cent, the purpose of which was to finance initiatives for improvement of agriculture and welfare of farmers; this was over and above the Swachh Bharat Cess imposed at the rate of 0.5 per cent on all taxable services only eight months earlier. Imposing taxes is always a problem politically, but surcharges and cesses do not invite that much attention or debate; whenever the Centre wanted money, cesses and surcharges provided a ready and easy but economically inefficient solution.

Under the crushing weight of the multiplicity of these taxes and the tyranny of tax inspectors who descended on industry and business premises, businesses and industries were gasping for breath. Add to it the harassment inflicted on the transporters at the border check post of a state. Any truck or commercial transport carrying and delivering goods across the country had to stop at the border check gates, which are veritable dens of corruption, to pay these taxes and accompanying bribes. The truck movements would thus be inevitably delayed, often when the demanded bribe was not paid immediately. Millions of trucks pass these check gates of the states and UTs every day, and were made to wait for hours at the border posts, delaying their movements and hence inter-state trade and commerce, and keeping economic growth of the country in suspended animation.

The distortions caused by the cascade of taxes and entry barriers were indeed suffocating to businesses and industries, and hence unfriendly to the helpless consumer. An example will make things clear. Before GST, the Union government had the authority to impose Central Excise Duty (CED) on the production or manufacture of any commodity save alcohol for human consumption and non-narcotic-containing medicinal preparations which were within the state's powers. The First Schedule to the Central Excise Tariff Act, 1985, determined the rates of CED on different commodities, classified under different categories of goods and covered under different sections of the schedule subdivided into chapters, each dealing with a particular class of goods. In addition, wherever there were inter-state sales of goods, a Central Sales Tax (CST) originally at the rate of 4 per cent was additionally leviable on the commodity. Hair oil, like many other items, was attracting CED at 12.5 per cent. States were empowered to impose a tax on sales of any commodity within their territories. Thus, in West Bengal, the VAT on hair oil was levied at 14.5 per cent; in Maharashtra, it was attracting a rate of 13.5 per cent.

Suppose there is a manufacturer M of hair oils in Maharashtra. For every ₹1,000 worth of the manufactured finished product, that is, hair oil, he paid ₹125 as CED to the Union government at 12.5 per cent; so he collected ₹1,125 from the buyer. If the buyer B happens to be registered within Maharashtra, B paid ₹151.88 as VAT to the state government at 13.5 per cent. The effective rate of VAT was thus hiked from 13.5 per cent to 15.18 per cent, and the product became costlier to that extent. If M sold it to a registered dealer in West Bengal, he had to collect CST from him, since CST was payable by the selling dealer who made the sale in the course of inter-state trade or commerce. The product price was hiked due to tax, even though the factor cost of production had not undergone any change.

Now it was despatched by a truck to West Bengal to the second seller W. He had to pay the entry tax at the border of each intervening state the truck passed through, and finally when the consignment entered the state of West Bengal (West Bengal subsequently abolished the entry tax on goods even before the introduction of GST). In West Bengal, the oil, whose price was already much higher than its original manufactured price, attracted a higher sales tax (VAT) of 14 per cent. So the final price of the commodity became even higher, but at each of the intermediate stages, the price had been artificially hiked, since no value was added to the product at any stage.

It was distortions of this kind that were playing havoc with industry and commerce, trade and businesses and hindering the seamless growth of the economy. The distortions were, in fact, much more pronounced and hurtful to the economy prior to 1986. Before 1986, even the CED of final product included elements of CED paid on its input components, besides a CED imposed on the CEDs already paid on these inputs. For example, say, for manufacture of hair oil, one needed inputs such as coconut oil and perfume, each of which attracted CED at specified rates when procured by the manufacturer of hair oil from the market, which added to the cost of the finished product. The final product, hair oil, was thus priced at cost plus mark-up, which was the element of profit earned by the manufacturer, and this price again was subjected to a CED. But the cost of the product had already included the elements of CED paid on its inputs; hence, the final price paid by the buyer equalled cost of the final product (which included CED on inputs) + mark-up on final product + CED on [cost of final product + mark-up on final product]. The CED paid on final product thus included not only the CEDs on the inputs paid earlier but also the CED on those CEDs. This was a classic example of the cascading effect of payment of tax upon taxes. The more the number of intermediary stages or inputs required in manufacture, the more would be the price-augmenting effect of this cascading, without adding any value to the product.

The first time this situation was attempted to be addressed was in 1986–87, when a concept of MODVAT (modified VAT) was introduced by the then finance minister, Mr V. P. Singh, in the Budget. That probably was the first step towards GST, as yet unconceived. The MODVAT was suggested as early as 1978, when the Indirect Taxation Enquiry Committee headed by Mr L. K. Jha, a former governor of the Reserve Bank of India (RBI; 1967–70), had made out a case for a change in the taxation structure by moving to a tax based on the successive value additions bringing in the concept of input tax credit. MODVAT permitted manufacturers of excisable goods to avail credit of duty paid on the inputs procured and used in or in relation to the manufacture of final products and to utilise such credit towards the duty liability on final goods. Thus, the purpose of MODVAT was clearly the avoidance of the cascading effect of taxes—multiple taxation on inputs as well as final products.

MODVAT was introduced with effect from 1 March 1986 in respect of a select number of commodities. The coverage was limited to 37 chapters out of a total of 91 chapters of the Central Excise Tariff. With effect from 1 March 1987, the coverage was extended to all commodities except petroleum products, textiles, tobacco, cinematographic films and matches. These excluded commodities accounted for a sizeable amount of the total excise revenue, amounting almost 50 per cent of the revenue from CEDs. The coverage was gradually expanded over the subsequent years, and by 1994–95, MODVAT had been extended to cover almost 85 per cent of the total Union excise revenues of the country. Finally, the 1994–95 Union Budget extended MODVAT to include petroleum products (excluding high-speed diesel [HSD] oil) and capital goods. The next Union Budget expanded its scope further, leaving out only a few items such as matches, cinematographic films, textiles, tobacco and HSD oil. MODVAT primarily allowed manufacturers to obtain instant and full reimbursement for excise duty paid on components and raw materials, bringing down the price of the final product substantially.

The Beginning of History

In the history of independent India, July 1991 was perhaps the most eventful month in terms of significance and profundity of impact. It was only in July 1991 that India finally shed its baggage from the past and took active steps to attain independence from the stifling state controls that had stymied the nation's growth for decades. It was in July 1991 that India had finally buried the disastrous legacy of Nehruvian socialism that had hitherto restricted the nation to a Hindu rate of growth ever since Independence and kept its people depressed in endemic and abject poverty while flaunting a socialistic pattern of society whose commanding heights were guarded by the sentinels of a public sector defined by cronyism, patronage, pilferage and inefficiency. We came back from the brink of a certain impending disaster, from being perilously close to becoming a failed state.

Since the mid-1980s, the country had been sinking deeper and deeper into an economic quagmire, primarily because of the continued worsening of its balance of payments position, triggered by an overvalued currency. Gulf War of 1990–91 exacerbated the crisis by swelling the import bills and dwindling our scarce foreign exchange reserves. Nehruvian economics of deficit financing led to escalating fiscal deficits which rose to 8.4 per cent of GDP by 1990–91. Inflation ranged over 12 per cent, and internal debt alone rose to 53 per cent of the GDP. India's external debt increased to US$72 billion from only US$20.5 billion in 1980, making India the third largest debtor nation after Brazil and Mexico. By June 1991, foreign exchange reserves fell to only US$600 million, or only two weeks equivalent of imports, and the prospect of defaulting on its external balance of payment obligations was looming ominously over the nation.

To escape the humiliating prospect of sovereign default, a desperate government had to secure an emergency loan of US$2.2 billion from the IMF by pledging almost its entire stock of 67 tons of gold reserves as collateral. To complete the humil iation, the IMF insisted on physical transfer of this gold, and RBI had to airlift 47 tons of gold to the Bank of England and the remaining 20 tons to the Union Bank of Switzerland. While this gold was being transported to the airport, the carrier van broke down, creating widespread panic. As a chartered plane ferried the precious cargo to London during the last 10 days of May 1991, an outraged nation and its hapless leaders were jolted out their deep slumber after 44 years. The Chandra Shekhar government that presided over this crisis collapsed shortly afterwards, and on 21 June 1991, P. V. Narasimha Rao took over as prime minister, with Dr Manmohan Singh as his finance minister. What followed has made the country what it is today. As the *New York Times* had reported on 29 June 1991,

> Mr. Rao, who was sworn in as Prime Minister last week, has already sent a signal to the nation—as well as the IMF—that India faced no 'soft options' and must open the door to foreign investment, reduce red tape that often cripples initiative and streamline industrial policy.[13]

It has been revealed that irrespective of the government that was to assume power, the reforms nevertheless would have been launched then. The then Chief Economic Advisor Mr Deepak Nayyar, and Mr Singh's predecessor, Mr Yashwant Sinha, both had confirmed that any finance minister would have read the same Budget speech in June 1991.[14] Dr Singh was fortunate to have his name inscribed in golden letters in the annals of India's destiny. In that eventful month of July of 1991, the rupee was devalued by 7 per cent and again by 11 per cent within the first three days. On 9 July, the Prime Minister addressed the nation, highlighting the need for reforms and promising to remove the cobwebs that hindered the economy. A New Industrial Policy and a path-breaking Budget defining the course of reforms the country was to embrace were presented together on 24 July.

It was actually Prime Minister Narasimha Rao, also the industry minister, who was the real architect of liberalisation. It was his industrial policy that had actually freed the economy from the suffocating License and Permit Raj architecture of the Nehruvian socio-economic philosophy and polity, built around a complex labyrinth of licenses, permits and controls that dictated

---

[13] Bernard Weinraub, 'Economic Crisis Forcing Once Self-Reliant India to Seek Aid', *The New York Times*, 29 June 1991. http://www.nytimes.com/1991/06/29/world/economic-crisis-forcing-once-self-reliant-india-to-seek-aid.html

[14] *The Times of India*, 'Manmohan and I Even Had the Same Speech', *The Times of India*, 24 July 2016.

every facet of our production and distribution, setting up entry barriers at every stage, and built a strong bias towards state ownership of the means of production. It viewed all private enterprises with extreme suspicion and believed in the domination of public sector over every economic activity. It abhorred international trade and erected tariff barriers to prevent India's integration into global economy which in its myopic vision was capitalist and hence repugnant. It had infinite trust in the wisdom of its redoubtable bureaucrats and Planning Commission members to control and direct the market forces towards India's growth.

The defined objectives of the New Industrial policy were to liberalise industry from all regulatory devices such as licenses and controls, enhance support to the small-scale sector, increase competitiveness of industries, ensure running of public enterprises on business lines and ensure rapid industrial development in a competitive environment. The cornerstones of this policy were (a) abolition of all industrial licensing, irrespective of the level of investment except for certain industries related to security and strategic concerns; (b) de-reservation of industries for public sector and allowing private sector in all areas save three—arms and ammunition, atomic energy and rail transport; until then, public sector had exclusive reservation over as many as 17 sectors; (c) disinvestment of public sector and their restructuring by giving them more autonomy, closing sick units and reducing government stake in them to 26 per cent or less; (d) free entry to foreign direct investment (FDI) and foreign technology for modernisation, and providing products and services of international standards, through a new FDI policy; and (e) abolition of MRTP[15]

---

[15] Under the Monopolies and Restrictive Trade Practices (MRTP) Act, 1969, all firms with assets of ₹25 crore or more were required to take permission from the Government of India for carrying out business. The limit of ₹25 crore was known as MRTP limit and was later raised to ₹50 crore in 1980, and then to ₹100 crore in 1985.

clearance for large industries and liberalising industrial location approvals.[16]

There were many other facets of the reforms process, and each of these contributed to the creation of a competitive industrial climate, built around the private and not the public sector by unleashing their immense energy, innovation and entrepreneurship to create wealth and job for millions, and by attracting financial capital from across the seven seas. The most pronounced and visible impact of the economic reforms unleashed in July 1991 has been a drastic fall in our poverty ratio, a dramatic improvement in our growth rates and a miraculous increase in the inflow of foreign capital and consequent built-up of our foreign exchange reserves. The story is known and documented too well to merit any further repetition here, but India's journey to real freedom was only about to begin. The journey will still be long and arduous, and it has not ended yet, as no journey ever does. As Allama Muhammad Iqbal wrote,

Sitaron se aage jahaan aur bhi hain

Har ek maqam se agay maqam hai tera

Hayat zauq-e-safar ke siwa kuch aur nahin.

(Unexplored worlds lie beyond the stars and your destination lies still beyond. Life is nothing but an endless journey.)

---

[16] Govind Bhattacharjee, 'Twenty Five Years After', *The Statesman*, 3 August 2016.

Chapter Two
At the End of a Long Journey

The First Halting Steps

The July 1991 Budget presented by Dr Manmohan Singh was a landmark event for the Indian economy. The Budget for 1994–95 was another milestone, because in that Budget, for the first time in our country's economic history, service tax was introduced on three select services to widen the indirect tax base. The service sector, so far untaxed, was contributing 40 per cent of GDP. Acting upon the recommendations of Dr Raja Chelliah Committee on tax reforms, Dr Manmohan Singh introduced in the 1994–95 Budget service tax at the rate of 5 per cent on only three select services: telephone services, non-life insurance and stockbroking.

Dr Singh had declared on that occasion,

> This Budget is inspired by a firm conviction that India has all the material and human resources to be a front-ranking nation of the world. We are on the threshold of a new century, indeed a new millennium. There are tremendous opportunities, provided we have the wisdom and foresight to seize them. There are also immense dangers if we falter or appear indecisive.

The Finance Act, 1994–95, defined the word 'service' to mean

> Any activity carried out by a person for another for consideration and includes a declared service, but shall not include (a) an activity which constitutes merely (i) a transfer of title in goods or immovable property, by way of sale, gift or in any other manner; or (ii) such transfer, delivery or supply of any goods which is deemed to be a sale within the meaning of clause (29A) of article 366 of the Constitution; or (iii) a transaction in money or actionable claim; (b) a provision of service by an employee to the employer in the course of or in relation to his employment; (c) fees taken in any Court or tribunal established under any law for the time being in force.

The coverage of the service has since been expanded year after year to include almost all services by 2012–13, save a few items in the Negative List that attracted no service tax liability, with consequent phenomenal increases in the revenue in successive years as shown in Table 2.1.

Tax on services gave a boost to the revenue collection, and the government could lower the tax rates and rationalise the tax structure with greater vigour in respect of all taxes. In 1997, the 'Dream Budget' of Mr P. Chidambaram, who was then the finance minister in H. D. Deve Gowda's United Front government, could thus slash the peak customs duty from 50 per cent to 40 per cent, with further simplification of tax structure.

Meanwhile in 1994, a study was undertaken by a team from the National Institute of Public Finance and Policy, New Delhi, headed by Amaresh Bagchi on 'Reform of Domestic Trade Taxes in India: Issues and Options' at the instance of the Ministry of Finance, Government of India. The objective of the study was to design a possible system of VAT for India on which the Centre and the states could agree to reform our 'chaotic and complex system of domestic trade taxes'. Schedule VII to the Constitution has fragmented the power of indirect taxation, distributing it between different levels of government,

Table 2.1: Expansion of Service Tax Network

Financial Year	Number of Services Brought Within the Tax Net	Revenue (₹ crore)
1994–95	3	407
2003–04	62	7,891
2004–05	75	14,200
2011–12	119	97,509
2012–13	Negative List Regime with Effect from 1 July 2012[a]	132,518
2013–14	do	154,778
2014–15	do	167,969
2015–16	do	211,414

Source: Budget documents and finance accounts of the respective years.

Note: [a] In terms of Section 66B of the Finance Act, 1994 (Service Tax Act as amended by the Finance Act, 2017), a service tax was leviable on all services provided by a person to another for a consideration other than the services specified in the Service Tax Negative List which was specified in Section 66D of the Finance Act, 1994. In all, there were 17 heads of services in the Negative List which included postal and agricultural services; services of the RBI; betting, gambling and lottery; transportation; and funeral services.

and hence devising a scheme of VAT needed to bring the Centre and the states together. As the team had recognised in the beginning, it was 'no mean task'. It believed that a VAT based on the guiding principles of neutrality, simplicity and equity could provide a solution to most of the ills of the present system, which was termed as 'archaic, irrational and complex'—in fact, 'the most complex in the world'.

It is interesting to note that many features of the present GST were identified in the report way back in 1994 itself. It realised that 'If common market is to grow, *the tax should adhere strictly to the principle of destination'* and clearly stated that

In exploring the possibilities of introducing VAT in India, one has to think of a dual system in which both the Centre and the

> States share the consumption tax base in a mutually acceptable arrangement.... Under such a system, there would be a common base for both Central and State VATs.[1]

It went on to add that

> The only feasible option seems to be a dual system in which the VAT is levied by the two levels of government independently within the existing constitutional framework. This would be possible if the MODVAT now operating through the excise tax system is made into a full-fledged manufacturers' VAT and the States also adopt a destination-based harmonized system of VAT in place of the chaotic sales taxes operating now.

The main elements of the reform as identified in the report included the transformation of MODVAT into a full-fledged manufacturer-level VAT with sufficient widening of the base so as to include all goods produced, manufactured or imported and a few selected services, provision for full and immediate credit of input duty to registered manufacturers and producers for all raw materials and parts used in manufacturing and rationalisation of the rates to introduce a structure of not more than three rates at the most and their eventual convergence into a uniform rate. The report recommended three rates (10 per cent, 15 per cent and 20 per cent) which along with (non-rebatable, non-sharable) excises on a few commodities and tax on selected services should protect the existing revenues of the Centre and the states. It worked out the revenue-neutral rates for five states—Andhra Pradesh, Gujarat, Maharashtra, Rajasthan and Tamil Nadu—within a range of 9.5 per cent and 13.1 per cent.

---

[1] 'Reform of Domestic Trade Taxes in India: Issues and Options: Report of a Strudy Team, 1994', NIPFP, New Delhi. Available at: http://www.nipfp.org.in/media/pdf/books/BK_39/Reform%20Of%20Domestic%20Trade%20Taxes%20In%20India%20Issues%20And%20Options.pdf (accessed on 12 December 2017).

For the state VAT, it recommended to convert sales taxes into VAT by moving over to a multi-stage system of sales taxation with rebate for tax on all purchases with only minimal exceptions, gradually extending the tax base to include all goods with minimal exceptions, and services which are integral to the sale of goods. Input tax credit was to be allowed for all raw materials and parts, consumables, goods for resale, and production machinery and equipment. Side by side, tax administration needed to be modernised with a high degree of computerisation. Harmonisation of the rates will naturally call for agreement among states and also the Centre, for which purpose and for achieving a continuing coordination between the Centre and the states so vital for success of such path-breaking reform the report suggested the setting up of a VAT Council of states as a mechanism for 'bringing all states together and ensuring their active participation', which will provide expertise, identify common tax base and establish common procedures to integrate the taxes.

The complexity of the issues, the prevailing political scenario and demands of the fractious coalition politics, especially since states were involved, were making consensus difficult. Again in 1999, the Vajpayee government focused upon the unfinished agenda of tax reforms, driven by its Finance Minister Mr Yashwant Sinha. In July 2000, an Empowered Committee of State Finance Ministers (EC) was set up by the Government of India under the chairmanship of Dr Asim Dasgupta, the then finance minister of West Bengal, with finance ministers of Karnataka, Madhya Pradesh, Maharashtra, Punjab, Uttar Pradesh, Gujarat, Delhi and Meghalaya as members.[2] The objective of the EC was to steer the process forward by bringing the

---

[2] Subsequently, state finance ministers of Assam, Tamil Nadu, Jammu and Kashmir, Jharkhand and Rajasthan were also notified as the members of the EC. In August 2004, the Government of India decided to reconstitute the EC with state finance/taxation ministers of all states as its members.

states and the Centre on the same platform, and to monitor the implementation of uniform floor rates of sales tax by states and UTs. It was to guide the states in phasing out of the sales tax-based incentive schemes, and to lay down the milestones and methods by states to switch over to VAT. Now finally, displaying a true spirit of cooperative federalism so rarely seen in India, the Centre and the states agreed to put an end to the sales tax war and settle for uniform floor rates for various commodities with effect from January 2000.

Launch of VAT was announced with effect from 1 April 2002, but it could only be launched with effect from 1 April 2005 due to severe resistance from traders, especially in the BJP-ruled Delhi and a few other states. In his Budget speech for financial year 2005–06, the then finance minister, Mr Chidambaram, had hoped: 'In the medium-to-long term, it is my goal that the entire production–distribution chain should be covered by a national VAT (value added tax), or even better, a goods and services tax, encompassing both the Centre and the States'.

VAT was expected to address the problem of taxing inputs at multiple levels along the supply chain and halt the competition among states to attract investment by offering economically unsustainable incentives. Every commodity passes through different stages of production and distribution before finally reaching the consumer, with some value added at each stage of the production and distribution chain; VAT is a tax on this value addition at each stage—it is a consumption tax (CT) borne by the final consumer. A dealer collects tax on his sales from the consumer, retains the tax paid on his purchase and pays the balance to the government. VAT is instead a multi-stage tax system with provision for collection of taxes paid on purchases at each point of sale, but at any stage along the supply chain, it is levied only on the value addition that occurs at that stage instead of levying them on value addition that has already occurred, which is claimed as input credit.

Tax evasion was as rampant then as of now. At that time, state governments used to collect around ₹85,000 crore by way of state sales taxes and further over 20,000 crore by way of CST. Most of it used to accrue from sales tax on petroleum, liquor, iron and steel, and cement companies. Rough estimates pointed to evasion of taxes amounting to as much as 50 per cent—almost equalling the volume of taxes actually collected. VAT was designed to make accounting more transparent, cut trade barriers and boost tax revenues by curtailing evasion.

While 20 states launched VAT with a rate of 12.5 per cent on 1 April 2005, 8 major states, 5 ruled by the BJP, besides Tamil Nadu, Uttaranchal (now Uttarakhand) and Uttar Pradesh, postponed its implementation, but would follow suit soon. Traders across the country welcomed the new regime with a three-day nationwide strike. Big industry organisations welcomed it and lobbied aggressively for its implementation, while small businesses, particularly retail traders, raised protests against it.

VAT came with several rates, a nil rate for basic items, 1 per cent for highly expensive items such as gold and silver, 4–5 per cent for most goods of daily consumption and a general rate of between 12 per cent and 15 per cent for goods which cannot be segregated and put under any of the aforementioned cate gories and for 'sin' goods such as liquor and cigarettes. The CST on inter-state sales was to be phased out over a period of three years beginning April 2007, reducing its rate by 1 per cent every year from the existing 4 per cent, with payment of adequate compensation to the states by the Centre. It was reduced in two years to 2 per cent in June 2008. However, no further reduction took place, leaving it ultimately to be subsumed in GST.

The Long Road to Freedom

In January 2004, the Parliament passed the Constitution (Eighty-eighth Amendment) Act, 2003, amending Article 270 and Seventh Schedule to the Constitution and inserting Article

268A to explicitly allow the Centre to tax services. Traditionally, the Centre had powers to tax the manufacturing of goods. The eighty-eighth amendment extended these powers to all services, including the services of trading and retailing of goods, enabling the Parliament to formulate the principles for levying, collection and sharing of these taxes with the states. From April 2000, MODVAT was renamed as CENVAT (central VAT). By 2002–03, all goods were covered by CENVAT; in 2004–05, service taxes were also added to CENVAT for the purpose of availing credit of service tax paid on the services by providers.

Meanwhile, the macroeconomic situation in the country was turning grave due to the continually rising trend of fiscal deficits over the years. Fiscal deficit is the gap between government's resources and expenditure, which has to be bridged by borrowing of one kind or the other. Heavy borrowing leads to greater indebtedness and high interest burden, which acts as a serious drag on future resources, and sets off a chain of undesirable economic consequences. By the turn of the century, the problem of high fiscal deficits was seriously upsetting the macroeconomic stability of the economy resulting in soaring inflation, leading to reduced consumption and crowding out of the private sector investment, rising unemployment and falling standards of living. It was becoming essential to institute a robust fiscal discipline framework. Revenue deficit was a very important contributor to the fiscal deficit, and the governments were unable to keep it within control due to their rising social welfare expenditure. To ensure intergenerational equity in fiscal management and long-term macroeconomic stability by eliminating revenue deficits and to bring in transparency and accountability in fiscal management, the Government of India enacted the Fiscal Responsibility and Budget Management Act (FRBMA) in 2003, which indeed was a landmark event in our fiscal history. Soon all the states would follow suit, prodded by the Twelfth Finance Commission. In fact, this would bring most states from the brink of certain financial disasters as they were irretrievably sinking into a viscous debt trap, from which they would not have been able to rescue themselves without the help of Twelfth Finance Commission's debt reliefs tied to the FRBMA. Under the FRBMA, both the Centre and the states were required to wipe out revenue deficit and cut fiscal deficit to 3 per cent of GDP by 2008–09, enforcing much needed fiscal discipline and prudence. The original form of the FRBM Bill had several other numerical fiscal targets as well, which were discarded during the process of passage of the Bill

> [That was intended to remove] fiscal impediments in the effective conduct of monetary policy and prudential debt management consistent with fiscal sustainability through limits on the Central Government borrowings, debt and deficits, greater transparency in fiscal operations of the Central Government and conducting fiscal policy in a medium-term framework.[3]

A Task Force was appointed under the chairmanship of Dr Vijay Kelkar, the then advisor in the Ministry of Finance on the implementation of FRBMA. The Task Force pointed out that the existing system of taxation on goods and services was inchoate, distortionary and inequitable, and suffered from many serious inherent problems. To overcome these problems, it suggested a comprehensive GST which should be a simple, transparent and efficient system of indirect taxation of goods and services in an integrated manner, as the distinction between goods and services was increasingly getting blurred. Introduction of a GST to replace the existing tax structure with multiplicity of central and state taxes was imperative in the emerging economic environment to help establish a common market throughout India, widen the tax base, unify and integrate indirect taxes, improve the revenue productivity of domestic indirect taxes and enhance welfare through efficient resource allocation.

---

[3] The Gazette of India, Controller of Publications, Government of India Press, 26 August 2003.

It identified, like the Amaresh Bagchi Study Team, the problems with the existing taxation of goods and services,

> The tax base is fragmented between the Centre and States. Services which make up half of GDP are not taxed appropriately. In many situations, the existing tax structure has cascading effects, where moving to a full VAT system has not yet taken place. These difficulties have led to substantial distortions, where the tax revenues from a few sectors are disproportionate, and the choice of production technologies and inputs in the country has become distorted. The existing flaws in tax policy have induced a malfunctioning tax administration. These problems have manifested themselves in terms of a poor buoyancy of excise collections, which has led to a low Tax/GDP ratio. More importantly, this has been a factor leading to slow growth of the manufacturing sector, and employment, in the country.[4]

To overcome these problems, it suggested that the

> VAT principle should be comprehensively used to tax the consumption of almost all goods and services in the economy. There is a need for the Centre and the States to come to an agreement on this fundamental issue. The Task Force proposes a 'grand bargain' whereby States will have the power to tax all services concurrently with the Centre. Consequently, both the Central and the State governments would exercise concurrent but independent jurisdiction over common or almost common tax bases extending over all goods and services, and in both cases, going upto the final consumer.[5]

In clear and unambiguous terms, it stated that

> The introduction of the GST at both Central and State levels should be accompanied by the withdrawal of all cascading taxes

---

[4] 'Report of the Task Force on Implementation of Fiscal Responsibility and Budget Management Act, 2003', Ministry of Finance, Government of India, July 2004, pp. 5–6.

[5] Ibid., p. 6.

such as Octroi, Central Sales Tax, state level sales taxes, Entry tax, Stamp duties, Telecom license fees, turnover taxes, tax on consumption or sale of electricity, taxes on transportation of goods and passengers, etc. This removal of inefficient and distortionary taxes would constitute a major milestone for reforms in Indian public finance.[6]

Calling this scheme a 'major milestone for the modernisation of India's indirect tax system', the Task Force estimated that

[It was likely to] lead to additional gross tax revenues from taxation of goods and services of 2 percentage points of GDP in 2008–09. Of this, roughly 0.6 percent of GDP would be transferred to the States, assuming existing formulas for resource sharing. This increase in the Tax/GDP ratio is central to the plan proposed in this report for achieving the FRBM targets.[7]

Thus, we see that most of the structural elements for a pan-India GST were laid down by 2004 itself. Indeed, as already mentioned, in his budget speech for financial year 2005–06, the then finance minister, Mr Chidambaram, had stated his goal of covering the entire production–distribution chain by a national VAT or a dual GST involving both the Centre and the states. The question is why then it took us so long to institutionalise such a system. Actually, the complexities of our fiscal federal structure demanded a gradual, incremental and politically consensual approach.

A proposal to introduce a national-level GST was first mooted in the Budget Speech for 2006–07, in which Mr Chidambaram had said,

It is my sense that there is a large consensus that the country should move towards a national level Goods and Services Tax (GST) that should be shared between the Centre and the

---

[6] Ibid., p. 7.
[7] Ibid.

States. I propose that we set April 1, 2010 as the date for introducing GST. World over, goods and services attract the same
rate of tax. That is the foundation of a GST. People must get
used to the idea of a GST. Hence, we must progressively con-
verge the service tax rate and the CENVAT rate.

Since the proposal involved reforming and restructuring of
the indirect taxes levied not only by the Centre but also by
the states, the responsibility of preparing a design and road
map for the implementation of GST was assigned to the EC.
In April 2008, the EC submitted a report titled 'A Model and
Roadmap for Goods and Services Tax (GST) in India' containing
broad recommendations about the structure and design of GST.
Based on the inputs from the Government of India and states,
it released its first discussion paper on GST on 10 November
2009. In order to take the GST-related work further, a joint
working group consisting of officers from the central as well
as the state governments was constituted. This was further
divided into three subgroups to work separately on draft legislations required for the introduction of GST, process/forms
to be followed in GST regime and development of IT infrastructure needed for the smooth functioning of the proposed GST
system. In addition, an empowered group for development of
IT systems required for GST regime was set up under the chairmanship of Dr Nandan Nilekani.[8]

After 2009 Lok Sabha elections, Mr Pranab Mukherjee
became the finance minister in the UPA II government. In the
Budget Speech for 2009–10, he declared that 'The broad con-
tour of the GST Model is that it will be a dual GST comprising
of a Central GST and a State GST. The Centre and the States will
each legislate, levy and administer the Central GST and State
GST, respectively'. In the same year, the terms of reference of

---

[8] Information bulletin no. LARRDIS (EF) 2014/IB-11, dated December 2014
issued by Lok Sabha.

the Thirteenth Finance Commission were broadened to include GST. In its report for the period 2010–15 submitted in December 2009, the commission devoted a full chapter, Chapter 5, of their report to GST, laying down a complete road map for its roll-out in what it called a 'Grand Bargain'. Elements of this 'Bargain' included a dual model GST to be levied at a single positive rate on all goods and services with seamless transfer of tax credits across different tax jurisdictions in the country. The central GST (CGST) would subsume all related indirect taxes and cesses: CED and additional excise duties, service tax, additional customs duty (countervailing duty), all surcharges and cesses, while the state GST (SGST) portion would subsume most state taxes: VAT, CST, entry tax whether in lieu of octroi or otherwise, luxury tax taxes on lottery, betting and gambling, entertainment tax, purchase tax, state excise duties, stamp duty, taxes on vehicles, tax on goods and passengers, taxes and duties on electricity and all state cesses and surcharges. Highlighting the benefits of such a tax, it said,

> Adoption of such a model GST would make India a dynamic common market and also result in generation of positive externalities. Despite lower levels of taxes, the revenue of the Union and the states will be buoyant. Subsumation of all major indirect taxes will result in removal of inefficient taxes. Our manufactures will become more competitive and consequently exports will grow.

> Provision of seamless transfer of input tax credits across all transactions will avoid tax cascading, eliminate double taxation and improve resource allocation. It will foster a common market across the country, reorient supply chains and remove the present bias towards backward integration. Further, it will also inhibit tax induced migration of investment. It will, thus, support the growth of lagging but resource-rich regions. A single rate across all goods and services will eliminate classification disputes and make tax assessment more predictable. The harmonisation of tax assessment, levy and collection procedures

across states proposed under the GST will reduce compliance costs, limit evasion, enhance transparency and improve collection efficiency.[9]

It also prescribed an objective compensation mechanism to provide reassurance to both the central and state governments, along with operational modalities, a binding agreement between the Centre and the states, with provisions for disincentives for non-compliance and an implementation schedule.

A study was conducted by the National Council of Applied Economic Research, a respected economic policy research institute, at the behest of the Commission, which estimated that the implementation of a comprehensive GST across goods and services will enhance the nation's GDP by between 0.9 per cent and 1.7 per cent, which it thought would lead to efficient allocation of the factors of production, with a consequent fall in the overall price level. Exports would gain by 3.2–6.3 per cent and imports by 2.4–4.7 per cent. It estimated the GST tax base at ₹31 lakh crore, and the consequent revenue-neutral rate at 11 per cent (5% for CGST and 6% for SGST). It suggested the single positive GST rate of 12 per cent (5% for CGST and 7% for SGST) other than exports.

Referring to the Finance Commission report, the finance minister in the Budget speech of 2010–11 stated, 'It will be my earnest endeavour to introduce GST along with the DTC in April, 2011', deferring it by one year from the earlier-promised date.

Conquering the Final Frontier

The passage of the GST Bill was anything but smooth. On 22 March 2011, Mr Pranab Mukherjee introduced the Constitution (One Hundred and Fifteenth Amendment) Bill in the Parliament

---

[9] Report of the Thirteenth Finance Commission, Volume 1, p. 70.

to give concurrent taxing powers to the Union and states for instituting the GST framework, including creation of a GST Council to recommend harmonised tax rates and a GST Dispute Settlement Authority. The Bill was referred to the Standing Committee on Finance headed by Mr Yashwant Sinha, which submitted its report in 2013. All through, the BJP-ruled states, led by Gujarat and Madhya Pradesh, kept up fierce opposition, as did Tamil Nadu. But the UPA government failed to get the proposed law passed by the Parliament until the dissolution of the 15th Lok Sabha, and the Bill automatically lapsed in 2014. However, the GSTN, the backbone of the proposed new taxation structure, was promoted after a committee headed by Mr Nandan Nilekani recommended it, and a non-profit, non-government private limited company was incorporated in the name of GSTN in 2013–14 as a special-purpose vehicle set-up by the government. Its duty was primarily to provide the IT infrastructure and services to the central and state government(s), taxpayers and other stakeholders for implementation of GST.

The Bill was reintroduced as the Constitution (One Hundred and Twenty-second Amendment) Bill, 2014, in the 16th Lok Sabha by the NDA government in December 2014. Majority of NDA in the Lok Sabha ensured smooth passage of the Bill in the Lower House in May 2015, but it was a different story in the Upper House, where the UPA led by the Congress still enjoyed the majority; they tried every trick up their sleeves to disrupt the proceedings and to block the passage of the Bill, so that the BJP cannot run away with the credit of finally launching a historical and path-breaking reform which had the potential of changing the economic landscape of the country and which was actually conceived by the Congress. It wanted to cap the rate of GST at 18 per cent and to incorporate this rate in the Bill itself. The government did not agree, because if the rate became a part of the Constitution amendment, to change it in future if necessitated by any contingency or circumstance would require another amendment which might not be easy to bring. But the antics of the Congress did not succeed because of the prevailing political situation.

First, some Congress-ruled states, like Karnataka, supported GST. By then, Mr Amit Mitra, the finance minister of West Bengal, was heading the EC, and West Bengal Chief Minister Ms Mamata Banerjee had extended full support to GST. Second, BJP was adroitly isolating the Congress even in the Rajya Sabha. The Bill was referred to a Select Committee of the Rajya Sabha on 14 May 2015 for submission of its report by the end of the first week of the upcoming monsoon session in July, during which the government planned to move the Bill and seek its passage in the Rajya Sabha.

A Constitutional Amendment Bill needed a two-thirds majority in each House of Parliament, to be ratified by at least half the total number of states, or 15 states. A string of losses in assembly elections after 2014 resulted in dwindling strength of the UPA led by the Congress in the Rajya Sabha, which fell down to 71 and for the first time ever, behind the BJP-led NDA's strength of 74. Now BJP started seeking the support of the regional parties aggressively—from Trinamool Congress, BJD, JD(U), Dravida Munnetra Kazhagam (DMK), Rashtriya Janata Dal (RJD), SP, Bahujan Samaj Party (BSP), Telangana Rashtra Samithi (TRS) and about a dozen nominated members. Congress was thus becoming isolated in the House, and its opposition was becoming irrelevant. Further, and after the May 2016 assembly election results in four states, the Congress' rule has got restricted to just 6 of the total 29 states. After the GST Bill is passed, it has to be ratified by half the number of states, or 15. Thus, the NDA-ruled states alone could ensure ratification of the Bill, without even seeking out the UPA-ruled states or even the non-NDA, non-UPA governed states.

In these circumstances, the Congress had no option but to relent or risk becoming irrelevant, perceived as being opposed to a game-changing reform which it had only initiated. The session of the Parliament had seen lot of turmoil that monsoon. The delay was also creating an environment of uncertainty not only for the domestic industry but was also sending signals to the global investors who wanted to invest in India that there was lack of consensus in the Parliament on economic reforms. But by the end of that turbulent and stormy July of 2016, the government was finally able to bring the Congress and the Left on board, who were opposing the Bill. Congress dropped its insistence of capping the rate to be fixed in the legislation, and yielding partly to their demands, the government had agreed to four key amendments, including dropping the proposal for 1 per cent levy by manufacturing states such as Gujarat, Maharashtra and Tamil Nadu. The others included mechanism for dispute-redressal which was made clearer by tweaking the language, full compensation for five years to states in case of revenue loss in lieu of abolition of additional 1 per cent extra levy incorporated earlier at the behest of manufacturing states, as well as the principle on which the revenue-neutral rate would be determined. On 3 August 2016, the Rajya Sabha unanimously passed the GST Bill, renumbered as the One Hundred and First Constitution Amendment Bill,[10] in a rare show of convergence among parties on a question of national interest and paving the way for establishing a common market for the entire country under a single unified tax regime.

The amended Bill was passed by the Lok Sabha on 8 August 2016 and, after ratification by the states, received Presidential assent on 8 September 2016. On 12 August 2016, Assam became the first state to ratify the Bill. By 9 September 2016, except Jammu and Kashmir, Karnataka, Kerala and West Bengal, all the states had ratified it. Jammu and Kashmir did

---

[10] The Bills are numbered as and when they are passed. It implies that at least 21 Constitution Amendment Bills were still pending before the Parliament on that day.

not hitherto have any service tax, but its legislature passed the GST Bill in July 2017, by which time all states had not only ratified the Bill but also passed their respective SGST Bills.

The Dynamics of GST

So how will GST work now? As the EC explains, GST is a 'tax on goods and services with comprehensive and continuous chain of set-off benefits from the producer's point and service provider's point upto the retailer's level'. It is a tax only on the value addition at each stage, and through the input tax credit mechanism, a supplier at each stage can set-off the GST paid on the purchase of goods and services during all earlier stages. The final consumer thus pays only the GST charged by the last dealer in the supply chain. The cascading effect is thus totally eliminated, and the final net burden of tax on goods will come down (Table 2.2).

Being controlled by IT network, with online filing of return and payment of taxes, the system also becomes transparent and efficient, which in due course will make way for wider coverage of tax base and improved compliance, leading to higher generation of revenues. Once revenues increase, the government may be in a position to lower the tax rates. As the prices fall, exports become more competitive. But most of all, there will be a level playing field for all stakeholders throughout the country with uniformity in tax rates and uniform procedures across the length and breadth of the country in respect of goods and services, reducing the administration and compliance costs in general.

The administration of the CGST would lie with the Centre and that of SGST with the states. The CGST and SGST will be paid to the accounts of the Centre and the states separately, and taxes paid against CGST can be taken as input tax credit for CGST only, to be utilised only against the payment of CGST at later stages. The same principle will also apply to SGST,

Table 2.2: Input Tax Credit in the Supply Chain and Avoidance of Cascading

Stage of Supply Chain	Purchase Value of Input	Value Addition	Value at Which Supply Goods and Services Made to Next Stage	Rate of GST (%)	GST on Output	Input Tax Credit	Net GST = GST on Output – Input Tax Credit
Manufacturer	100	30	130	10	13	10	13 – 10 = 3
Wholesaler	130	20	150	10	15	13	15 – 13 = 2
Retailer	150	10	160	10	16	15	16 – 15 = 1

Source: http://empcom.gov.in/content/20_1_FAQ.aspx (accessed on 27 November 2017).

preventing cross-utilisation of input tax credits. The taxpayer will submit periodical returns to both GST authorities.

Both taxes will be levied simultaneously on every transaction of supply of goods and services, except for the exempted ones and for transactions below the threshold limits. Further, both would be levied on the same price or value unlike VAT which is levied on the value of the goods inclusive of CENVAT. While the location of the supplier and the recipient within the country is immaterial for the purpose of CGST, SGST would be chargeable only when both the supplier and the buyer are within the same state.[11]

The new tax regime is going to transform almost every sector and is likely to be indifferent to the budget of the *aam aadmi* (common man) as can be seen from Table 2.3.

Table 2.4 shows the tax levels before and after the launch of GST in respect of a few commodities of general use by almost everyone as well as other commodities. It confirms that by and large, GST will be consumer-friendly, and especially so for consumers at the bottom of the pyramid. It is to be remembered that in the earlier regime, the effective tax rates which were compounded by many taxes imposed on a product, were often not visible. ·

Unrealised Potential, Undiminished Complexities

Thus, after 30 years, and having been negotiated by 9 prime ministers and 12 finance ministers, GST was finally a law, but as we shall see, it is far from the simple, single-rate, unified law it was supposed to be, covering all commodities in the country, making India truly a one-tax common market. There were

---

[11] http://empcom.gov.in/content/20_1_FAQ.aspx (accessed on 30 November 2017).

Table 2.3: Impact of GST on Common Man's Budget (₹)

Average Household Size 2 + 2 Expense Items	Monthly Household Income: ₹50,000				Monthly Household Income: ₹80,000			
	Budget (₹)	Pre-GST (Tax Rate %)	Post-GST (Tax Rate %)	New Budget	Budget (₹)	Pre-GST (Tax Rate %)	Post-GST (Tax Rate %)	New Budget
EMI non-Home Loan, Consumer Durables, Medicines, Mobile and Insurance Bill	25,000	15	18	25,750	39,500	15	18	40,685
Rent	19,000	—	—	19,000	25,000	—	—	25,000
EMI for Vehicle	5,500	31	28	5,335	9,500	31–48	28	9,500
Education	5,000	—	0,18a	5,100	1,000	—	0,18	10,200
Entertainment	2,400	22	18	2,304	8,500	22	18	8,160
Vegetables, Milk, Fruits, Bread, Basmati Rice, Atta	2,000	0	0	2,000	3,500	0	0	3,500
Tea, Coffee, Butter, Biscuit, Curd, Ice Cream, Sweets, Juices	850	5–38	12–28	808	1,000	5–38	12–28	950
Toiletries	500	36–40	12–28	440	700	36–40	12–28	662
Total	**41,250**			41,167–41,737, with rent and home loan respectively.	**72,700**			72,907–73,657, with rent and home loan respectively.

Source: Constructed from a graphic published in the *Times of India*, 30 June 2017.[12]
Note: aWhile tuition is tax-free, canteen and additional facilities attract 18 per cent GST.

---

[12] Rachel Chitra, 'What GST Will Change, What You Could Change', *The Times of India*, 30 June 2017.

Table 2.4: New Tax Rates vis-à-vis Old (%)

Items	GST Rate	Previous Effective Rate	Items	GST Rate	Previous Effective Rate
Items of Common Use: Cheaper			**Items of Common Use: Dearer**		
Hair Oil	18	26	Branded Butter	12	5
Toothpaste	18	26–28	Ghee and Cheese	12	5
Soap	18	26–28	Agarbatti	12	0
Spectacles and Lenses	12	18.5	Jam and Jellies	18	12
Steel Utensils	5	18.5	Chocolates	28	25–26
Namkeens	12	26	Cakes and Pastries	18	11–15
Toothpowder	12	26	Instant Coffee	28	26
LED Light	12	26	Sanitary Napkins	12	5–6
Broomsticks	5	18	Razor	28	26
Milk and Beverages	12	26	Shaving Cream	28	26
Mineral Water	18	26–28	Hair Cream	28	26
Bread	5	5–12.5	Dyes	28	26
Leisure			**Industrials**		
Movie Tickets (>₹100)	28	22–23	Cement	28	25–27
Online Movie Tickets (<₹100)	28	0–50	Petroleum Coke and Bitumen	18	27.5
Five-star Restaurants	28	18	Coal	5	11
AC/Alcohol-serving Restaurants	18	22	Paints	28	16
Economy Air Ticket	5	6	Building Bricks	5	18.5

Hotel Room (₹2,500–7,500)	18	28
Hotel Room (>₹7,500)	28	28–30
Consumer Durables		
AC	28	25–26
Washing Machine	28	25–26
Coolers	28	23–24
Refrigerators	28	24–27
Cell Phone	12	6
Real Estate		
Sale of Under-construction Units	12	5.5
Vehicles		
Bicycle	12	18.5
Two-wheelers	28	27–30
Small Car	28	27–30
Large Car/SUVs	28	43–51
Ceramic Tiles	28	26
Furniture	28	26
Adhesive	18	25–28
Lubricant	18	25–28
Fertilisers	5	18.5
Utility Bills		
Telecom	18	15
Insurance/Loans	18	15
Other Items		
Coaching Class	18	15
Jewellery	3	2.5
Leather Bags	28	6
Wrist Watches	28	26
App-based Cabs	6	5
Rubber Tyres	28	18.5

Source: Constructed from a graphic 'Get Price Wise on New Tax' published in the *Economic Times*, 1 July 2017.[13]

Note: These rates have been changed substantially after the 22nd and 23rd meetings of the GST Council. Now only 50 luxury items and 'sin' goods like tobacco attract the highest rate of 28 per cent.

[13] *The Economic Times*, 'India's Tryst With Tariff', *The Economic Times*, 1 July 2017. Available at: http://epaperbeta.timesofindia.com//Gallery.aspx?id=01_07_2017_009_017_009&type=P&artUrl=Indias-Tryst-With-Tariff-01072017009017&eid=31816 (accessed on 12 December 2017).

several exemptions and multiple tax slabs which always give rise to classification problems and many other imperfections. As the BBC commented, GST, by itself, was 'no magic pill' and it was not going to be an 'easy journey'. 'Clearly, a successful GST in India will be a minor miracle', because 'No country of comparable size and complexity has attempted a tax reform of this scale'.[14] Also, as both the revenue secretary and chief economic adviser had asserted, no country could claim a flawless GST since inception, and constructive changes in complex systems are always incremental. GST in the form that it was implemented was no doubt far from the ideal, perfect tax one would have desired, but instead of waiting an eternity to design and implement a perfect system, it was much more pragmatic to start with an imperfect one and keep on correcting the glitches as and when they arise. In any case, it was far more perfect than 'our current patchwork quilt of taxes, which prevents India from being stitched into a single market', as economist Vivek Dehejia said.

The One Hundred and First Amendment Bill was only one of the many milestones to have been achieved before GST fully became operational. The date for its roll-out was initially decided to be 1 April 2017, but the rates of GST remained to be finalised by the GST Council and the complete operational infrastructure needed to be set up before launching GST. The roll-out date had to be finally postponed to 1 July 2017. Before that, all states had to pass their respective SGST Bills, and appropriate revenue-neutral rates had to be worked out. There were many uncertainties—it is not clear whether small businesses were fully geared for the new tax regime which was based largely on technology or whether the tax will stoke inflation if the rates were not worked out correctly. A higher than

---

[14] Soutik Biswas, 'Why India's GST Is One of the World's Most Complex Tax Reforms', BBC, 4 August 2016.

desirable rate could always stoke inflation. Some of the biggest beneficiaries were expected to be the populous, non-producing but high consuming states such as Bihar and West Bengal, while some of the losers were expected to be the industrialised states such as Gujarat or Maharashtra. Further, since it was a dual tax, both Centre and the states had to work in close coordination and agreement, and there was every scope that serious differences could easily crop up between them, either over the rates or over tax-sharing arrangements. Implementing of a complex new tax system is always fraught with high risks, and there was no mechanism available to insulate either the Centre or the states against these risks.

GST subsumed altogether 17 central and state taxes, besides 13 cesses. There would now be two taxes, the CGST and the SGST, replacing respectively the central and state indirect taxes. The dual model ensured that they would continue to be collected by the Centre and states respectively, and their sharing would be determined in a manner specified in the Acts. These two taxes will subsume the existing taxes and duties levied and collected by the Centre and states respectively (see Boxes 2.1 and 2.2). In addition, there will be an inter-state GST

Box 2.1: Central Taxes and Duties Subsumed in the CGST

1. Central Excise Duty
2. Additional duties of excise (goods of special importance)
3. Additional duties of excise (textiles and textile products)
4. Excise duty levied under the Medicinal and Toilet Preparations (Excise Duties) Act 1955
5. Service tax
6. Additional customs duty (countervailing duty)
7. SAD of customs
8. Central surcharges and cesses in the nature of taxes on goods/services such as cess on rubber, tea, coffee and national calamity contingent duty

Integrated GST will subsume CST.

Box 2.2: State Taxes and Duties to Be Subsumed in SGST

1. State VAT/sales tax
2. Entertainment tax (unless it is levied by the local bodies)
3. Luxury tax
4. Taxes on lottery
5. Taxes on betting and gambling
6. Tax on advertisements
7. Octroi
8. Entry tax
9. Purchase tax
10. State cesses and surcharges in so far as they relate to supply of goods and services

(IGST) which would replace the CST, and which would be the sum of CGST and SGST on a commodity or service, and would be levied on all supplies of goods and/or services in the course of inter-state trade or commerce. Import of goods or services would be treated as inter-state supplies, and thus it would be subject to IGST in addition to applicable custom duties. Exports would be zero-rated. The cesses and surcharges imposed on taxes that have been subsumed in GST will automatically stand abolished; these include the Krishi Kalyan Cess and the Swachh Bharat Cess levied on service tax, the education cess on excisable goods and other little known cesses such as those on tea, sugar and jute. Seven cesses will continue as they relate to customs or goods that are not included in GST. These include education cess, secondary and higher education cess on imported goods, and cesses on petroleum products and tobacco and tobacco products, which, though covered by GST, are still included in the Union List as excisable commodities. As many as 26 cesses levied by the Centre along with excise duty and service tax were earlier abolished to pave the way for GST.[15]

---

[15] *The Hindu*, 'Centre Abolishes 13 Cesses along with GST Rollout', *The Hindu*, 3 July 2017. Available at: http://www.thehindubusinessline.com/economy/policy/centre-abolishes-13-cesses-along-with-gst-rollout/article9747204.ece (accessed on 13 December 2017).

Acts were needed to be passed by the Parliament in respect of both CGST and IGST, and also a separate one in respect of GST in UTs, to give effects to the proposals relating to the subsumation of the aforementioned taxes. Even though there would be multiple legislations in respect of SGST, some uniformity would have to be maintained in respect of the basic features in each legislation as far as feasible such as chargeability of the tax, definition of taxable events and taxable persons, classification and valuation of goods and services, and procedure for collection and levy of the tax; otherwise, the purpose of dual GST itself would be defeated.

Some of the taxes that would continue as before under the new GST regime and have been kept out of the jurisdiction of the new tax regime are basic customs duty, property tax, stamp duty and registration fees, motor vehicle tax, electricity duty and a few commodities such as the highly lucrative and rent-seeking items such as alcohol for human consumption, petroleum and petroleum products oil. The most notable exception is the real estate sector (property tax,[16] stamp duty and registration fees). Real estate, in fact, is the highest absorber of black money and the commonest conduit of money laundering and benami transactions; without bringing this sector within the ambit of the new tax, it is not clear how the government's objective of reducing black money through GST could succeed. Alcoholic liquor for human consumption has been kept out of GST, and tobacco products would be subject to separate excise duty in addition to GST. Further, petroleum products shall continue to be taxed as per the existing laws and would be brought under the GST regime from a future date to be notified by the GST Council; presently, these are within the ambit of the GST regime, but with zero tax. Among the services, 87 services

---

[16] In most states, property tax is being levied by local bodies and not by the state government.

including some in the erstwhile Negative List of Services will remain exempted from GST, including education and health care services as well as services related to charitable activities.

Some opposition leaders have alleged that real estate and liquor have been kept out because 'influential people' and politicians run them and lobbied for these to be kept out as they invest their 'black money' in it. Truth may not be so simple, though the possibility of the pressure of the lobby groups, especially the powerful real estate lobby, could not be rejected outright, because bringing this sector under the ambit of GST would have been immensely beneficial on many counts. Restrictions on credit utilisation could have been eliminated at a single stroke, since GST would automatically lower the tax burden on input items such as bricks, cement and steel, as input tax credits would be available for set off at various stages leading to the lowering of construction costs and consequent reduction in the real estate prices. It is argued that real estate being concerned with immovable property is neither a good nor a service within the scope of various sales tax and VAT acts of states, and thus cannot be covered under the GST. But this is only a definitional problem and could have been easily addressed to bring this vital sector under GST.

As the economy adjusts to the new tax regime, one can only hope that the real estate sector will be brought under GST, for without this, driving core sectors of the economy into a formal stream will always remain a chimera. This important sector, which today operates largely as non-formal and unorganised with considerable capacity for absorption of black money, cannot be kept out of the formal stream of the economy for long if we are to reduce corruption and eliminate black money, which are the stated goals of the present government. By formalising this sector, GST has the capability to improve transparency and efficiency of the real estate sector by making the supply chain smoother. Once this is brought into the formal stream, unscrupulous transaction will be minimised and tax compliance will go up significantly, resulting in possible further lowering of the tax burden. Margin in the hands of contractors/ developers will increase as a result of unification of taxes such as VAT, service tax, excise duty, entry tax and octroi now being paid on the inputs charged to them under the current system. Dynamics of a competitive market will force these benefits to be passed on to the end-consumers, driving down the pricing of real estate sector as a whole, boosting the ancillary industries as well through forward and backward linkages. The elements of construction costs which today go unrecorded will also be eliminated, minimising if not eliminating the use of black money.

By looking at the collections from stamp duty and registration fees by the states as depicted in Table 2.5, it can be seen that a substantial part of the own revenues of the states were being collected from the real estate sector alone, in spite of the significant evasions. Naturally, the states were reluctant to sacrifice

Table 2.5: Collections from Stamp Duty and Registration Fees by States: 2015–16

State	Collections from Stamp Duty and Registration Fees (₹ Crore)	Total Own Revenues of the States (₹ Crore)	Collections from Stamp Duty and Registration Fees as Percentage of State's Own Tax Revenues
Maharashtra	21,766.99	126,608.11	17.2
West Bengal	4,196.20	39,409.98	10.6
Karnataka	8,214.71	75,550.18	10.9
Gujarat	5,549.42	62,649.41	8.7
Punjab	2,448.98	26,690.49	9.2
Tamil Nadu	8,721.45	80,476.08	10.8

Source: Finance accounts of the respective states. For West Bengal, 2014–15 finance accounts figures have been used.

Table 2.6: State Excise Receipts from Alcohol: 2015–16

State	Excise Receipts from Alcohol in (₹ Crore)	Total Excise Receipts (₹ Crore)	Receipts from Alcohol as Percentage of Total State Excise Receipts
Maharashtra	12,021.10	12,469.56	96.4
West Bengal	3,962.06	4,015.12	98.7
Karnataka	15,163.85	15,332.88	98.9
Punjab	4,605.31	4,796.45	96.0
Tamil Nadu	5,715.90	5,836.02	97.9

Source: Finance Accounts and Commercial Tax Departments of the respective states. Tamil Nadu figures have been sourced from Commissionerate of Prohibition and Excise, Chennai.

this rich source of revenues by completely migrating to VAT, in view of the uncertainties that characterise every such transition to a new tax regime, and also the fear of losing control over their own revenues in view of their rising fiscal deficits. Once successful implementation is able to address these apprehensions, they can be reasonably expected to be more amenable to future proposals for bringing this sector also under GST. The lobbying allegation thus gives a partial explanation at best.

The same considerations also apply to the liquor sector, which today is one of the most buoyant sources of state revenues, as seen from Table 2.6. Excise collections from alcohol alone constitute almost the entire receipts of state excise, and naturally the states were opposed to give up this source of revenue which often financed their revenue expenditure as well as welfare schemes for the targeted groups of voters. Revenues from excise accounted for substantial volumes of the total own revenues of the states, next only to their collections from sales tax/VAT.

It may be noted that state excise is not the only tax a state collects from alcohol, it also collects significant amounts of VAT and CST on the sale of alcohol. Thus, Maharashtra collected ₹5,790.21 crore from VAT and CST, Punjab collected ₹239.54 crore, while Tamil Nadu collected a whopping ₹20,018.81 crore.

The GST Architecture

The One Hundred and First Amendment also provided for compensation to be paid to the states for loss of revenue arising on account of implementation of GST for a period which may extend up to five years; this necessitated the legislation of another Act of the Parliament. By June 2017, the Parliament had already passed all the four Bills necessary for implementing GST—CGST Bill, Integrated GST Bill, Union Territory GST Bill and GST (Compensation to States) Bill—after these were approved by the GST Council following clause-by-clause debates spread over as many as 12 meetings conducted over a period of 6 months. While states and UTs with their own legislatures, namely Delhi and Puducherry, enacted their own GST legislation for levying SGST, UTs without legislatures such as Andaman and Nicobar Islands, Lakshadweep, Dadra and Nagar Haveli, Daman and Diu and Chandigarh will be governed by the Union Territory Goods and Services Tax (UTGST) Act, 2017, for levying UTGST.

The One Hundred and First Constitution Amendment Bill amended Articles 269, 270, 271 and 279. Since GST will subsume several taxes, the Seventh Schedule to the Constitution of India had to be amended simultaneously (see Box 2.3).

Box 2.3: Amendment to Seventh Schedule

Union List
Entry 84: Duties of excise on manufactured products substituted by duties of excise on petroleum crude, HSD, petrol, natural gas, aviation turbine fuel and tobacco
Entry 92: Taxes on the sale or purchase of newspapers and on advertisements therein—omitted
Entry 92C: Service tax—omitted

State List
Entry 52: Tax on the entry of goods—omitted
Entry 54: Taxes on sale or purchase of goods substituted by taxes on petroleum crude, HSD, petrol, natural gas, aviation turbine fuel and alcohol
Entry 55: Taxes on advertisement —omitted
Entry 62: Taxes on luxuries, entertainment, betting and gambling, etc.—omitted

As regards distribution of the proceeds of the GST between the Union and the states, under the amended Article 269A(1), IGST will be levied and collected by the Union to be apportioned between the Union and the states in the manner as may be provided by the Parliament by law on the recommendations of the GST Council. Under Article 269A(2), the amount apportioned to a state will not form part of the Consolidated Fund of India, where all revenues are to be credited and from which nothing can be spent without Parliamentary approval. Thus, the part of IGST going to the states will not be votable by the Parliament. As per the amended Article 270(1A), the GST levied and collected by the Union, except the tax apportioned with the states under Clause 269A(1), that is, IGST, shall also be distributed between the Union and the states in the manner provided in Clause 269A(2). Article 271 of the Constitution which empowers the Parliament to increase any duties or taxes by surcharge for the purpose of the Union which it has no obligation to share with any state was always a sore point of contention between the Centre and the states. It has now been amended by providing an exception to GST, thus taking away the power of the Centre to levy any surcharge on GST for the purpose of appropriating it for Union's purposes. The net proceeds of additional tax on supply of goods shall be assigned to the states from where the supply originates.

The amended Article 279A provides for the constitution of a GST Council to examine issues relating to GST and make recommendations to the Union and the states on parameters such as rates, exemption list and threshold limits. The Council shall function under the chairmanship of the Union finance minister and will have the state union ministers as its members. It further provides that every decision of the Council shall be taken by a majority of 75 per cent votes. While discharging the functions conferred by Article 279A, the GST Council shall be guided by the need for having a harmonised structure of the tax and for the development of a harmonised national market for goods and services. The GST Council is also required to establish a mechanism to adjudicate any disputes between governments and also those arising out of its recommendations, a departure from the proposal of having a separate GST Dispute Settlement Authority as stipulated in the original Constitution (One Hundred and Fifteenth Amendment) Bill.

Further, an additional tax on supply of goods, not exceeding 1 per cent, in the course of inter-state trade or commerce shall be levied and collected by the Government of India for a period of two years or such other period as the GST Council may recommend, and such taxes shall be assigned to the states. Central government may, where it considers necessary in the public interest, exempt such goods from the levy of additional tax.

Petroleum products thus continue to be excisable by the Union and VAT-able by the states; similarly, alcohol remains excisable by the states. The reasons for this is not difficult to fathom. The states are already apprehensive of losing a part of their sales tax and excise revenues. These revenues from the petroleum sector constituted the most vital constituent in the states' total collections (Table 2.7), and they could not be persuaded to give up their claims over the largest chunk of their revenues, at least not as yet. Even for the Centre, it would amount to a loss of a substantial source of their revenues. As of 2015–16, for the central and the state governments, the petroleum sector yielded ₹4.18 lakh crore of revenue (from Union excise and state sales tax/VAT and other tax and non-tax sources),[17] almost amounting to 3 per cent of the GDP. Thus, it

---

[17] The Union government gets royalty on oil and gas produced from the offshore fields, whereas the state governments get royalty from onshore fields. Some licence fee for carrying out exploration is also payable to the Union government in the case of offshore fields and to the state governments in the case of onshore fields. Cess at the rate of ₹2,500 per tonne is levied on production from nominated and pre-New Exploration and Licensing Policy

Table 2.7: Sales Tax Receipts from Petroleum and Petroleum Products: 2015–16

State	Receipts from Petroleum and Petroleum Products in 2015–16 (₹ Crore)	Total Receipts from VAT/ Sales Tax (₹ Crore)	Receipts from Petroleum and Petroleum Products as Percentage of Total VAT Receipts
Maharashtra	15,642.51	69,660.82	22.5
West Bengal	5,869.00	24,021.91	24.4
Karnataka	8,131.59	40,448.63	20.1
Gujarat	7,920.59	44,091.05	18.0
Punjab	4,113.97	15,856.64	25.9
Tamil Nadu	10,114.89	57,522.03	17.6

Source: Finance Accounts and Commercial Tax Departments of the respective states.

was natural that neither the states nor the Centre would agree to bring this sector under the GST, and thereby risk losing their discretion to increase the taxes even when the crude price has been falling worldwide. If the compensation mechanism works out well, at a later stage, these commodities might be expected to be integrated into the GST; in fact, petroleum is still covered under GST with a zero rate that can be increased once the GST Council decides with 75 per cent majority.

As regards the compensation to states, the GST (Compensation to States) Act, 2017, provides that the Parliament may, by law, on the recommendation of the GST Council, provide for compensation to the states for loss of revenue arising on account of implementation of GST (after taking into account the collections against SGST) for a maximum period of five

---

(NELP) fields. While oil public sector undertaking (PSUs) pay cess and royalty on production from the nominated fields, companies that produce from pre-NELP fields pay cess, royalty and profit petroleum. In the case of NELP fields, companies pay profit petroleum and royalty.

years. The Act further provides that for the purpose of calculating the compensation amount in any financial year, 2015–16 will be reckoned as the base year, from which revenue will be projected at a growth rate of 14 per cent per annum for the five-year period. The base year tax revenue will consist of the states' tax revenues from state VAT, CST, entry tax, octroi, local body tax, taxes on luxuries, taxes on advertisements, etc. However, any revenue among these taxes arising related to supply of alcohol for human consumption, and certain petroleum products, will not be accounted as part of the base year revenue. The amounts will be as certified by the Comptroller and Auditor General (CAG) of India. To fund the compensation to states for revenue losses under GST, a clean energy cess has been levied on coal, lignite and peat production at the rate of ₹400 per tonne.

The threshold limit for exemption of GST has been fixed at ₹20 lakh (₹10 lakh for special category states), while the compounding threshold limit has been fixed at ₹75 lakh (₹50 lakh for special category states) which will not be available to interstate suppliers, service providers (except restaurant service) and specified category of manufacturers.[18]

However, working out the rates was proving to be tenuous. Different states had different viewpoints, and there was divergence between the views of manufacturing states and consuming states. After its 14th meeting in May 2017, the GST Council, the apex body comprising the Centre and the states set up to decide on GST issues, could finalise a four-tier tax structure comprising five rates—nil rate for most basic items; 5 per cent (2.5 + 2.5), 12 per cent (6 + 6), 18 per cent (9 + 9) and 28 per cent (14 + 14) for GST (CGST + SGST)—while the highest slab was pegged in the law at 40 per cent (20 + 20). It fitted over

---

[18] Composition scheme contains an option for a registered taxable person having turnover less than the prescribed limit to pay tax at a lower rate subject to certain specified conditions.

1,200 goods and 500 services in the tax brackets of 5 per cent, 12 per cent, 18 per cent and 28 per cent. In its 15th meeting held in June 2017, a 3 per cent rate for GST was fixed for precious metals like gold and ornaments.

In order to ensure that the benefits of the new tax system are actually passed on to the consumer by the dealer, by exercising its powers under the CGST Act, 2017, the central government promulgated the Anti-profiteering Rules, 2017, in respect of GST and created an authority known as the National Anti-profiteering Authority. The authority will determine whether any reduction in the rate of tax on any supply of goods or services or the benefit of the input tax credit has been passed on to the recipient by way of a commensurate reduction in the prices by a registered dealer. The authority is empowered to order reduction in prices, return to the recipient the amounts not passed on by reduction in prices along with interest at the rate of 18 per cent, impose penalty as prescribed under the Act and may even cancel the registration of the delinquent dealer under the Act. Similar anti-profiteering provisions exist in Malaysian and Australian GST systems.

GST is an entirely new and rather complex tax regime, and its provisions will therefore require many clarifications for businesses. For this purpose, the GST Act provides for setting up of an Advance Ruling Authority (AAR). An advance tax ruling is a written interpretation of the tax laws by the tax authorities issued to a taxpayer who requests for such clarification on the law or procedure relating to his tax liability before starting his proposed business activity. The ruling given by the AAR is binding on the applicant as well as tax authorities and can obviate long drawn and expensive litigations that might later arise. While the procedure of applying for advance ruling is inexpensive, simple and expeditious, the mechanism provides certainty and transparency to a taxpayer with respect to a contentious issue which has the potential of dispute with the tax administration. The advance ruling given by AAR can be appealed before an Appellate Authority for Advance Ruling (AAAR) within a specified timeframe.

At the heart of the GST system sits the GSTN as the technology backbone for GST, powered by the software built by Infosys. The GSTN is a not-for-profit private limited company which was incorporated in March 2013 with an authorised capital of ₹10 crore only, which are shared by the Government of India (24.5%), all states and UTs of Delhi and Puducherry and the EC (24.5%), the balance 51 per cent being contributed by private financial institutions.[19] Expenses of the GSTN are to be shared equally between the central and the state governments.

The GSTN is responsible for creating the IT infrastructure to migrate nearly 90 lakh entities registered with the Excise and Service Tax departments, and with VAT departments in the states, onto one single digital platform. Each of the states has a different format for VAT, and to integrate all these into a common compatible structure before migrating data has truly been a monumental task. The GSTN has validated the existing business entities from the old databases using their permanent account numbers (PANs) and found 90 per cent of them active. Almost 30 per cent of these entities registered showed a turnover of under ₹5 lakh, which meant that they could still claim the VAT credit, but lying below the GST threshold turnover of ₹20 lakh has no liability to pay the tax. With more registrations expected, the GSTN will expand its capacity gradually to 1.5 crore entities. Each taxpayer is allotted a 15-digit GST Identification Number GSTIN which will be essential for any transaction. The new entities are required to register online. Over time, the GSTN is expected to be the largest commercial, real-time taxation software anywhere used globally.

---

[19] Ten per cent each by HDFC, HDFC Bank, ICICI Bank, NSE Strategic Investment Co. and LIC Housing Finance Ltd (11%).

The GSTN is to manage the entire IT system of the GST portal, which is the master database of GST, which will provide all necessary services to the taxpayers—from registration to payment of taxes and filing of returns. From registration to invoicing, filing of returns, payments and refunds, everything in GST will be handled by the GSTN through a GSTIN which is a unique number based on a taxpayer's PAN. Every taxpayer will receive the GSTIN once he is registered with the GSTN common portal. The GSTN is equipped to handle 30,000 lakh invoices per month, apart from return filing for about 90 lakh taxpayers. The GSTN portal will maintain all tax details which can be used by the government to track every financial transaction pertaining to GST. The GSTN will provide a common interface for the taxpayers while at the same time creating a shared IT infrastructure between the Centre and states. The infrastructure is extremely complex and sophisticated; without this, it would not have been possible to create an efficient settlement mechanism for the Centre and states, especially in relation to the IGST for inter-state trade, considering the huge volume of pan-India transactions. IGST will also be levied on all imports. A change from the present regime would be that the states where imported goods are consumed will now gain their share from the IGST paid on imported goods. A working model of IGST, as released by the Press Information Bureau, is shown in Figure 2.1.

Is This the Long-awaited Dawn

Has the new tax regime really benefited the consumer in concrete terms, or is the whole thing only a propaganda blitz without any visible benefits, a criticism that has been levelled in relation to the hugely disruptive demonetisation exercise of the last year? Table 2.8 shows the taxes a dealer had to pay in the erstwhile tax regime for selling a Windows operating system

Figure 2.1: IGST Model: Working Example

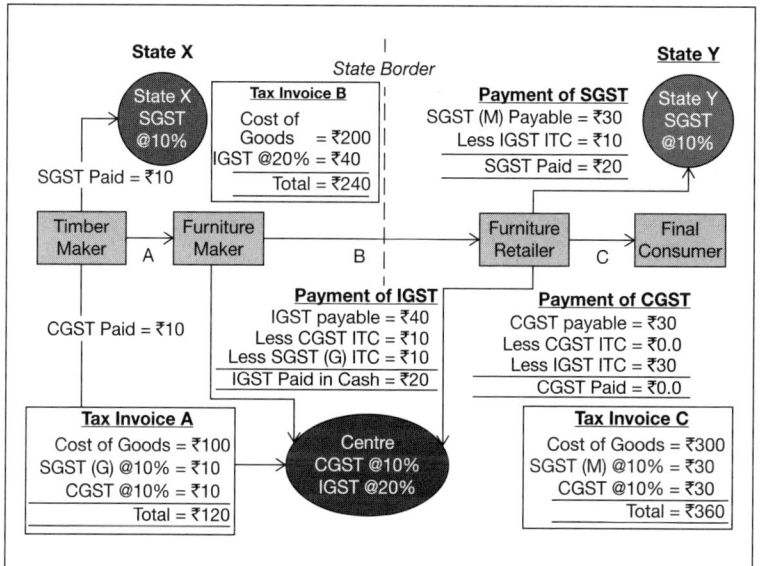

Source: http://pib.nic.in/newsite/PrintRelease.aspx?relid=148240 (accessed on 22 September 2017).

software and the tax impact post GST. We can see that there is a net 3.5 per cent reduction in price for the consumer. The same logic is applied to most commodities of common use by all.

Any change, to qualify as a game-changer, will necessarily be disruptive, as the president, while launching GST on the midnight of the new dawn, had said,

> GST is a disruptive change. It is similar to the introduction of VAT when there was initial resistance. When a change of this magnitude is undertaken, however positive it may be, there are bound to be some teething troubles and difficulties in the initial stages. We will have to solve these with understanding and speed to ensure that it does not impact the growth momentum of the economy.

Table 2.8: Pre-GST Taxes vis-à-vis Post-GST Situation (₹)

	Pre-GST	Manufacturer's Price (MP)		Post-GST
Cost Price (CP) to Distributor	2,866			2,866
	3,385	Excise duty (ED) on MP (12.5%) + VAT on (MP + ED: 5%)	GST on MP (18%)	3,382
Sale Price (SP) for Distributor (CP + Margin)	3,724	Margin (10%)	Margin (10%)	3,720
Cost Price to Retailer (CPR) (SP + Total Taxes at Distributor Stage)	4,469	VAT on SP (5%) + ST on SP (15%)[a]	GST on SP (18%)	4,390
Sale Price for Retailer (RSP) (CPR + Margin)	4,916	Margin (10%)	Margin (10%)	4,829
Price to Customer (RSP + Total Taxes at Retailer Stage)	5,899	VAT on Retailer's SP (5%) + ST on Retailer's SP (15%)	GST on Retailer's SP (18%)	5,698

Source: Constructed from a graphic published in the *Times of India* on 4 August 2016.[20]

Notes: Net VAT/GST Payable by Retailer (after Claiming ITC) + Net ST Payable by Retailer (after Claiming ST Credit).

[a] Net VAT/GST payable by distributor (after claiming VAT ITC + Net ST payable by distributor (full amount payable since no credit was available).

---

[20] *The Times of India*, 'How Almost Everybody Gains from GST', *The Times of India*, 4 August 2016. Available at: http://epaper-beta.timesofindia.com//Gallery.aspx?id=04_08_2016_016_008_012&type=P&artUrl=GOOD-SENSE-TAX-04082016008&eid=31808 (accessed on 12 December 2017).

As the Economic Survey 2015–16 pointed out, GST 'is a reform perhaps unprecedented in modern global tax history' which has the potential to push India's GDP by 1 per cent–2 per cent. The success of 'Make in India' and many other government initiatives may well depend on the success of GST. Shifting from a source-based taxation system to a destination-based system in a complex country like India is in itself a daring step. If managed successfully, and in the true spirit of inclusive and cooperative federalism, it may propel India from a US$1.3 trillion economy to a US$10 trillion economy within a decade.

An air of expectancy as well as an air of apprehension surrounds the GST for reasons not difficult to divine. After 30 tumultuous years, a nationwide GST is at long last a reality that has the potential of integrating the US$2 trillion economy of the country with its 1.3 billion people into a single market to liberate its economy from its sad colonial vestiges and its ostentatious socialistic pretensions. Existence of trade barriers has so far kept the country divided into 29 autonomous economic zones, erecting formidable barriers to trade and commerce. GST has attempted to dismantle these barriers and transform the country into a single economic zone, with same rules prevailing everywhere. It is now far from perfect, but has been achieved through difficult negotiations and compromises and by arriving at a rare harmony between rival political parties. It is a bold experiment fraught with great risk, the risk of creative destruction. If it fails, the old regime will bounce back. But if we can collectively steer it into a shining success, it will stand out as a beacon of hope and resurgence and lead us to a better economic future. Then we will finally be able to shed the baggage of our past failures and emerge from the 'hesitations of history' to transform our economy into a vibrant and modern engine of growth. The resilience of the Indian nation has been put to test once again, and failure is no option. We have to successfully negotiate the transition and integrate ourselves fully into the world economy. Otherwise, we shall be left to lament, like what Faiz Ahmed Faiz wrote on the eve of our Independence,

Yeh daagh daagh ujaalaa, yeh shab gazidaa seher

Woh intezaar tha jiska, yeh woh seher to nahin....

(This dawn arrived stained and scarred, battered by the night. This was not the dawn we had all waited for.)

Chapter Three
Insights from the Travails of Other Pioneers

Another Dual GST at a Steep Price

Launching of GST in India was indeed a bold step fraught with high risks, as we have already observed. A radical economic reform can make and unmake governments anywhere. The most striking example of this is Canada, and the Canadian GST has many features in common with the Indian GST.

In January 1991, led by Prime Minister Brian Mulroney and Finance Minister Michael Wilson, Canada introduced a dual GST like India's for the first time in its history, replacing a highly unpopular 13.5 per cent Manufacturers' Sales Tax (MST) which was hurting its international trade and thwarting the manufacturing sector's ability to export competitively, and the government thought that the introduction of a harmonised GST would address this situation. The introduction of the GST in Canada was controversial and, as in India's case, far from perfect. Canadians had to cope with soaring inflation over the next two years which the government could not control. Mr Mulroney, the prime minister from 1984 through 1993, who led the first Conservative majority government in 26 years from 1984 to 1988 and then again led the government for a second time, had to pay a steep price for this. In the Parliamentary election of 1993, his ruling Progressive Conservative Party (PCP) which enjoyed a majority of 169 out of total 295 seats in the House of Commons got thoroughly trounced, its strength being reduced to a pitiable remnant of only two seats, in a most dramatic collapse of an elected democratic government anywhere in the world. The reason was the adverse economic consequences, real as well as perceived, flowing from the GST. The opposition Liberal Party under Jean Chrétien, which had promised to repeal the GST, won the 1993 election with a strong mandate. Although the PCP would recover somewhat and emerge stronger in subsequent elections, it remained the smallest party in the House of Commons until it disbanded itself permanently in 2004 and merged with the Canadian Alliance to form the Conservative Party of Canada.

But ironically, GST was not the sole villain in this election rout which was the result of a combination of various factors. The worldwide recession during the early 1990s had already resulted in progressive worsening of the government's deficits, and on top of this, Mulroney had cut taxes on businesses. As a result, annual budget deficits soared to a record Can$42 billion in 1993, and national debt rose dangerously close to the GDP. Rising debt levels weakened the Canadian dollar, and Canadian economy was entering a period of recession. Simultaneously, for meeting its zero inflation target, the central bank, Bank of Canada, started raising interest rates which further accentuated the ill effects of recession, further weakening the currency. GST could not raise the tax levels enough to have a positive impact on the deficits. The economic slump led to widespread public resentment, and GST became the object of public wrath, causing disastrous political fallout for the ruling party.

GST, as we have observed in the last chapter, is a disruptive reform and needs to be managed carefully. Managing disruption is never smooth and easy. There are bound to be hiccups, and these hiccups can prove to be very unsettling, both economically and politically. To be sure, GST is not a miracle cure for everything that ails the economy. Any transition to the GST regime needs to be managed very carefully.

Like in India, GST everywhere followed introduction of VAT. France was the first country to introduce VAT way back in 1954. As many as 160 countries today, including all OECD countries except the USA, have some form of VAT or GST. Many countries have introduced GST by harmonising the taxes on goods as well as on services, partially if not wholly, but very few of them have a federal structure—and hence the attendant complexities—like ours. Among the developed economies, the USA does not have any VAT or GST. The federal government in the USA is primarily funded by personal and corporate income taxes, and payroll taxes such as social security and Medicare, while states impose a sales tax at the subnational level. However, each of its constituent states has a different mixture of taxes on sales, income and property. Some of the countries which have harmonised the taxes on sales of most goods and services include, besides India, France and Italy, UK, South Korea, Japan, Singapore, Sweden, Hong Kong/China, Austria, Malaysia, Canada, Germany, Russia and Australia, the last six being federations besides India. The polity of the Canadian federation has many features very similar to those of the Indian federation, including the asymmetrical powers granted to certain provinces, and the GST systems of these two countries also share remarkable similarities. Canada, like India, follows a dual model of GST—federal as well as provincial—and both share a complex taxation structure where different systems of taxation coexist. Let us, therefore, examine the Canadian GST system first, and in somewhat greater details, before discussing the features and implementation of GST in a few more federal countries.

Canada is the second largest country in the world in terms of land area, but much of its territory is buried under the Arctic permafrost and hence has limited potential for human use. It is a federation whose history dates back to the nineteenth century. On 1 July 1867, the Dominion of Canada was born out of the union of the three British colonies of Canada, Nova Scotia and New Brunswick. Canada now has 10 provinces and 3 territories in the far north. Two of its provinces, Ontario and Québec in the east, form the heart of the federation, with more than half of Canada's population and housing three quarters of its industrial capacity. Prior to 1867, these two provinces used to constitute the western and eastern regions respectively of the then province of Canada. Among all the provinces, Québec enjoys a special status in many respects, like our special category states. Québec is predominantly Francophone and largely inhabited by Catholics, while Ontario is largely Anglophone and Protestant, like the other nine English-speaking provinces. Québec retains its control over language, culture and life, and enjoys substantial financial and political autonomy, unlike the other provinces of Canada.

The three northern territories—Northwestern Territory, Yukon Territory and Nunavut Territory—exercise powers delegated by the Federal Parliament, while municipal governments exercise powers delegated by the province or territory. The division of powers is outlined in the Constitution Act, 1867, which is the basis for the Canadian Constitution. Powers of taxation are shared by the federal and provincial legislatures as in India, in accordance with Sections 92(2) and 92(9) of the Constitution Act, 1867, and the Federal Parliament enjoys more powers of taxation with provincial taxation being rather restricted, again like in our country.

The Canadian tax system is also rather complicated, not unlike the Indian tax system. Initially Canada had a Federal Sales Tax (FST) at the manufacturing level, which was levied by the federal government. Being in the nature of a turnover tax, it was initially taxed at 1 per cent on all wholesale transactions. In 1924, this was replaced by a single-stage MST, levied only at the point of manufacture. This tax was far from popular, and its rate was gradually lowered to 1 per cent in 1930 with the intention of abolishing it in the next year, but before that Great Depression intervened. Instead of abolishing the tax, the soaring fiscal deficits led to an increase of its rate to 8 per cent in 1936, when it yielded 31 per cent of all federal revenues. The rate of the tax ultimately reached 13.5 per cent on most goods. It became the major source of revenue for the federal government, contributing about one-sixth of the total federal tax revenue in 1990. The depression had also led to the introduction of the first subnational sales taxes in Canada, with provincial retail sales taxes being imposed in Saskatchewan in 1937 and in Québec in 1940.[1]

The MST had many inherent inadequacies. Its base was rather narrow—covering only one-third of the total goods and services. Structurally it was complex, with many artificial distinctions between goods and services leading to frequent disputes. But the worst was its cascading effect; it taxed a host of inputs, caused many other distortions that affected the margins of traders, distributors, wholesalers, retailers, importers and exporters, and negatively impacted the entire gamut of business, trade and commerce. About half of the FST revenue came from taxes on inputs. All efforts to remove the deficiencies by reforming the tax from time to time proved futile and ineffective. At the subnational level, all provinces, except Alberta, already had a system of sales tax; these were imposed by the provincial governments at different periods until 1964.

---

[1] Richard M. Bird and Pierre-Pascal Gendron, 'Sales Taxes in Canada: The GST–HST–QST–RST "System"', 29 May 2009. Available at: https://www.researchgate.net/publication/228280890_Sales_taxes_in_Canada_The_GST-HST-QST-RST_system (accessed on 30 November 2017).

The three territories of Canada do not have any such territorial sales taxes.[2]

The Federal Sales Tax Review Committee appointed by the Liberal Federal Government in 1983 held that neither an improved manufacturer's tax nor a wholesale tax was the solution and instead suggested three options to consider: (a) a national retail sales tax, (b) a federal retail sales tax or (c) a federal VAT. The committee's recommendation was for the third option which would require the federal government to collaborate with the provinces for introducing and administering the tax. But nothing further was done to switchover to a new system, due to the perceived difficulties, especially for ensuring the necessary cooperation from the provincial assemblies which was considered a major obstacle, like in India.

In 1984, the Progressive Conservative government of Prime Minister Brian Mulroney was voted to power. In the late 1980s, it started pursuing the issue of sales tax reforms and declared its intention to replace this inefficient MST by a new federal value-added sales tax called the GST on all goods and services except food essentials, medical services, prescription drugs, day care services, residential rent, legal services and educational programmes. The GST was also to replace the Federal Telecommunications Tax of 11 per cent. The government wanted the new GST to be a nationally harmonised sales tax that would replace individual provincial sales taxes (PSTs), and both levels of government would share the revenues generated. The revenue-neutral rate for this GST was worked out at 9 per cent. But a large section of the Canadian population remained unconvinced, and there was huge opposition against it.

---

[2] Mahesh C. Purohit, 'Structure and Administration of VAT in Canada: Lessons for India', *VAT Monitor* (November/December 2001): 311. Available at: http://empcom.gov.in/WriteReadData/UserFiles/file/2001-16.pdf (accessed on 13 December 2017).

Efforts and negotiations for harmonising the provincial and national sales taxes proved unsuccessful, with provinces challenging the federal government's constitutional powers to introduce a tax in an area that was 'historically reserved for the provinces'. Finally, in 1989, the federal government announced its intention to implement a national sales tax, the rate of which would be lowered to 7 per cent from the originally proposed rate of 9 per cent, and go ahead even without the cooperation of the provinces. The following year, however, Québec signed an agreement with the federal government that transferred full responsibility for administration of the GST (in Québec) to the province.[3] It was introduced in the province with effect from January 1991, along with the rest of the country.

On 24 January 1990, the GST Bill was introduced in the House of Commons. All political parties strongly disapproved of the proposal. Their major concern was that the tax would prove to be regressive and would hit the poor harder than the rich. In the three days prior to the vote, 1.7 million Canadians had filled out GST protest cards. As CBC reported,

> Over the cries of hecklers in the gallery, members of Parliament voted on the controversial Goods and Services Tax bill. For eight long months, politicians have debated the necessity of the new seven per cent tax. The Conservatives have touted the tax as a deficit-busting tool, but critics say it will be hard on lower-income Canadians. On the bill's third and last reading, the House of Commons votes to pass it, 144 to 114.[4]

---

[3] http://www.cra-arc.gc.ca/tx/bsnss/tpcs/gst-tps/rts-eng.html (accessed on 30 November 2017); http://www.mapleleafweb.com/features/goods-and-services-tax-overview-history.html (accessed on 30 November 2017).

[4] CBC Digital Archives. Available at: http://www.cbc.ca/archives/entry/1990-canadians-to-face-more-taxes-with-the-new-gst (accessed on 30 November 2017).

Even three ruling party MPs voted against the government Bill and were kicked out of the Progressive Conservative caucus. In the Senate, however, the opposition Liberals enjoyed a 52–46 majority over the Conservatives, much like in our Rajya Sabha after the Constitution (One Hundred and Twenty-second Amendment) Bill was passed in the Lok Sabha. The Senate refused to pass the tax into law. To break the deadlock, on 27 September 1990, Mulroney took the unusual recourse to an obscure, little-known constitutional provision, Section 26 of the Constitution Act, 1867, to increase the number of Senators temporarily by eight, thus giving the ruling party a majority in the Senate. An angry opposition launched a filibuster—the delaying tactic of prolonged debate which obstructs progress in Parliament and prevents a vote but does not technically contravene the procedures—to delay the legislation. After more than two months of tense debates, however, on 13 December 1990, the GST legislation was passed in the Senate, and from 1 January 1991, the 7 per cent GST went into effect. It was expected to add Can$15 weekly to the budget of a family of four due to lower prices of goods and services, besides boosting exports significantly. The actual fall in prices of goods was much less, and as experts had rightly pointed out, prices take time to adjust in a market economy, and the effect of the GST could be seen only over time and not overnight.

Given the complexity of a dual tax system like the GST in a federal country, administrative and compliance costs were naturally high. There were also concerns about the potential distributional effects of the tax, especially when there was a raging controversy in the country over its free-trade agreement with the USA. GST thus became a major issue in the 1993 elections. As already stated, Liberals had won the 1993 elections with a huge margin. Voters sent 177 of their members to the House of Commons on 25 October. During the election campaign, they released its Red Book—their manifesto, in which they promised to replace the GST 'with a system that generates equivalent revenues, is fairer to consumers and to small business, and promotes federal–provincial fiscal cooperation and harmonization'. But after getting elected, they did nothing of that sort, partly because they realised that public finances were in a precarious condition, with mounting debts and soaring deficits. They found that the GST was a very important source of government revenues, and it could not be junked or replaced. Even ignoring the attendant political risks—one of their MPs, in fact, had voted against the government's first Budget and had to be expelled from the Liberal caucus and another had resigned—they retained the tax with a different name.

Initially, the Chrétien government attempted to restructure the tax and merge it with the PSTs in each province, but found it difficult under the Constitution as it would encroach upon the state's domains. They intended to call it the 'Blended Sales Tax' immediately, but opponents started calling it derisively as the 'BS (Bullshit) Tax'. The name was finally changed to Harmonised Sales Tax (HST) before its introduction. In 1996, the three small Atlantic provinces (New Brunswick, Nova Scotia, and Newfoundland and Labrador) agreed to replace their regional sales tax (RST) with VAT under the name of the HST, in return for a substantial initial payment from the federal government. In these provinces, it would combine the 7 per cent federal GST with the PSTs whose rate would fall from 10 per cent to 8 per cent, resulting in a combined rate of 15 per cent along with the federal GST on the same base. The HST would be collected by the Canada Revenue Agency (CRA) for remittance of appropriate amounts to the respective provinces. The new tax for these provinces went into effect on 1 April 1997.[5]

---

[5] David Murrell and Weiqiu Yu, 'The Effect of the Harmonized Sales Tax on Consumer Prices in Atlantic Canada', *Canadian Public Policy* 26, no. 4 (2000): 452.

The government initially claimed to have replaced the GST by the GST/HST, which was in fact the same and, unlike the 1991 GST in Québec, applied directly to the same base as the federal GST.[6] Later that year, Prime Minister Jean Chrétien apologised for reneging on his election promise to eliminate the GST. For over two and a half decades now, Canada, thus, administers not only a federal VAT but two distinct varieties of provincial VATs—the Québec Sales Tax (QST) and the HST in Québec. British Columbia and Ontario adopted the GST/HST model in 2010, and Prince Edward Island in 2013. British Columbia later repealed the tax.

GST again acquired renewed importance during the 2006 federal elections. The Conservative Party, led by Stephen Harper, promised to reduce the tax rate by 1 per cent, while Liberals promised lowering of income taxes instead. The election returned the Conservatives to power and they indeed reduced the GST rate to 6 per cent in their very first Budget in May 2006, which came into effect from 1 July that year. With effect from 1 January 2008, the rate of GST was further reduced from 6 per cent to 5 per cent which still continues. The lowering of the rate in 2008 was estimated to have caused a decrease in the government revenues by approximately Can$6 billion.

The difficult birth of the GST was partly due to the fact that most of the MST was invisible, while most of the GST became visible to the consumer. Under the GST/HST system, most goods and services are advertised at prices, and taxes are to be paid 'extra' and not included in the price like the MST, thus making taxes highly visible. The consumer who sees a product priced at Can$99 on a store shelf finds that he or she must pay Can$111.87 to take the product home, after paying 13 per cent HST. This is due to a Constitutional provision—Section 92(13) of the Constitution Act, 1867—that gave the provincial

---

[6] Bird and Gendron, 'Sales Taxes in Canada'.

governments jurisdiction over advertising and posting of prices, precluding the Parliament to legislate any act requiring prices to be advertised tax-included (except in areas of federal jurisdiction). The provinces chose not to require prices to include the GST, similar to their own PSTs.[7]

The Canadian Model

The GST is defined in law in Part IX of the Excise Tax Act of 1985. In Canada, the HST combines the GST and PST into a single sales tax. This changes the PST from a cascading tax system to a VAT like the GST. There are now three different models of sales tax prevalent among Canada's various provinces: Québec levies a VAT (QST); five provinces (Newfoundland and Labrador, Nova Scotia, New Brunswick, Ontario and Prince Edward Island) levy an HST, which is a combination of GST and state VAT, and all other provinces levy a PST, which is actually in the nature of RST. Québec thus administers both the federal GST and the provincial QST—in fact, it is the only province to administer the federal tax. While QST and HST cover most goods and services but not investment, PST is primarily levied only on goods with some exceptions. Some specified consumer products and goods for resale are exempted from the PST in most provinces, to mitigate distributional and other burdens, but usually these exemptions do not follow any rational, systematic pattern and vary widely from province to province. Most services remain exempt under PST, though many provinces have increasingly brought many services under the PST such as car repairs, hotel/motel accommodation, insurance premium, telephone, communication services, computer software, and labour services. 'Sin goods' such as tobacco and alcohol are taxed usually at higher rates in most provinces.

---

[7] David M. Sherman, 'Policy Forum: Tax-included Pricing for HST—Are We There Yet?', *Canadian Tax Journal* 57, no. 4 (2009): 846–48.

GST is levied on supplies of goods or services made in Canada and cover most products, except certain politically sensitive essential goods and services. The exempted (zero-rated) items include basic groceries, most agricultural and fish products, prescription drugs, certain medical devices,[8] inward/outbound transportation services, international flights, residential rents, health and dental care, educational services, day care services, music lessons, legal aid services and financial services (such as interest on loans, charges for accounts, credit card fees and commission on transactions in stocks or other securities); they also include most goods and services supplied by governments and sales made by small traders with annual taxable turnovers below prescribed limits, besides occasional sales (e.g., private sales of used cars). Exported goods and services are also zero-rated, while purchases by tourists (for taking goods out of Canada) are also zero-rated, if the amount paid exceeds a certain threshold. Tourists are allowed refunds of the tax paid on accommodation while in Canada. To avoid cascading, full amount of input tax credits are allowed for set-offs at subsequent stages, and the tax burden falls essentially on the final consumer. But the system is not invulnerable to frauds, and criminals have defrauded it by claiming GST input credits for non-existent sales by fictional companies.[9]

Institutions such as municipalities, academic institutions (including universities), schools and hospitals, collectively referred to as MASH sector, that only provide services and do not engage in sales but have to pay GST on their purchases, are allowed a partial rebate on the taxes paid by them, something like a partial zero rating. Individuals with low incomes

---

[8] GST/HST Memoranda Series ME-04-02-9801-E 4.2 Medical and Assistive Devices.

[9] 'Opening Statement to the Standing Committee on Public Accounts: Enforcing the Goods and Services Tax'. Office of the Auditor General of Canada, 19 March 2003, archived from the original on 18 February 2006.

are allowed GST rebates calculated in conjunction with their income tax.[10]

The HST is administered by the CRA as part of the GST, with no separate administration or accounting by businesses. Place-of-supply rules determine whether a particular supply of property or services should bear GST or HST, but all taxes collected by a business are remitted through one return with no breakdown. The federal government uses statistical economic data to determine how much of the tax collected by it is passed on to the provinces as their share of HST revenues.[11] The evolution of the sales tax regime in Canada is shown in Table 3.1 and the current rates in Table 3.2.

Many of the challenges being faced by us now had to be overcome by the Canadian system after the introduction of GST in 1991—both are dual systems in a federal set-up with the same base for federal and provincial revenues. Studies clearly point out to the success of GST in Canada, both for provincial economies and for consumers. It is generally acknowledged that,

For decades, academics had argued almost unanimously that one could not impose a standard invoice-credit destination-based value added tax (VAT) at the subnational level of government. Canada's almost two decades of experience demonstrates conclusively that this view is incorrect: not only can it be done, but it has been done, and done well. Moreover, Canadian experience also demonstrates that a federal VAT can work perfectly well in a country in which some subnational units have their own VATs, some have their own retail sales taxes (RSTs), and some have no sales tax at all. The facts are thus on the ground and visible: the Canadian system not only works but works fairly well.[12]

---

[10] https://www.topcafirms.com/index.php/white-paper/3787-canadian-gst-model (accessed on 30 November 2017); also: Purohit, 'Structure and Administration of VAT in Canada'.
[11] Sherman, 'Policy Forum: Tax-included Pricing for HST'.
[12] Ibid.

Table 3.1: Evolution of Sales Tax Regimes by Jurisdiction

Province	Introduction of RST/PST	Initial Rate (%)	Present PST Rate (%)	Conversion to HST	Remarks
British Columbia	1948	3	7	2010	Reverted to PST in 2013
Alberta	1936	2	—		Repealed in 1937
Saskatchewan	1937	2	6		
Manitoba	1964	5	8		
Ontario	1961	3%	8	2010	
Québec	1940	2	9.975		Converted to QST in 2012
New Brunswick	1950	4	11	1997	
Nova Scotia	1959	3	11	1997	
Prince Edward Island	1960	4	1	2013	
Newfoundland and Labrador	1950	3	12	1997	

Sources: 'Ultimate Purchasers Tax Act, SA 1936, Chapter 7'; 'An Act to Amend the Ultimate Purchasers Tax Act, SA 1937 (2nd Session), Chapter 6'; 'Taxation', *Encyclopedia of Saskatchewan*; Ontario Committee on Taxation, III, 212–13; 'Retail Sales Tax', Ministry of Finance (Ontario); 'Revenue Tax Rate History', Department of Finance, Energy and Municipal Affairs (PEI).

Table 3.2: Current Sales Tax Rates (October 2016) by Jurisdiction

Province	HST (%)	GST (%)	PST/QST (%)	Total Tax (%)	Remarks
Federal Level		5			Federal GST at 5% is applied throughout the country. Federal government also administers a PST in the HST provinces (total tax 15%)
British Columbia		5	7	12	PST applied to retail sales price, excluding GST
Alberta		5		5	
Saskatchewan		5	6	11	Same as British Columbia
Manitoba		5	8	13	Same as British Columbia
Ontario		5	8	13	Same as British Columbia
Québec		5	9.975	14.975	Applied to GST base plus GST
New Brunswick	15			15	
Nova Scotia	15			15	
Prince Edward Island	15			15	
Newfoundland and Labrador	15			15	

Sources: http://www.cra-arc.gc.ca/tx/bsnss/tpcs/gst-tps/rts-eng.html (accessed on 27 November 2017); http://www.rev-enuquebec.ca/en/entreprise/taxes/tvq_tps/historique-taux-tps-tvq.aspx (accessed on 26 September 2017); https://www.researchgate.net/publication/228280890_Sales_taxes_in_Canada_The_GST-HST-QST-RST_system (accessed on 27 November 2017); http://publications.gc.ca/Collection-R/LoPBdP/BP/prb0003-e.htm (accessed on 27 November 2017).

The First VAT–GST System in the World: The French Model and EU

France was the first country in the world to have introduced a VAT system way back in 1954. The VAT (French: *Taxe sur la Valeur Ajoutée*, TVA) is a tax on consumption which applies to goods and services located in France. It is included in the sale price of these goods and services. VAT in France is imposed only on the value added at each stage of production, distribution or marketing. As explained earlier, in a value-added system, the overall tax burden remains limited to the tax on the final price paid by the consumer, and all taxes paid on inputs during all the intermediate stages between the production and the final sale to the consumer of a product are offset through a system of input credits so that there is no tax on taxes; the cascading of taxes leading to artificial increases in prices without any addition of value is thus eliminated altogether. In France also, VAT is finally borne by the end-user since it is included in the sale price of products or services. At each intermediate stage, that is, every time there is a sale or purchase transaction, VAT is assessed on the value of goods or services supplied. The supplier charges VAT to the buyer of his goods/services and pays it to the government, minus the VAT on inputs paid by him to his own supplier in turn so long as he is not an end-user. Thus, only the value added to the product or service at each stage of production or marketing in the supply chain, through which the goods or services reach the buyer, is taxed and the overall tax paid to the government is the tax calculated on the final sale price that the consumer pays, and the final consumer knows how much VAT he/she is paying.

On 10 April 1954, VAT was introduced in France to replace its existing tax on production. The VAT was initially imposed only on goods and was aimed at large businesses, but it was gradually extended to include all business sectors including services by 1967, when the European Union (EU) also recommended a common VAT system, in order to establish a single market across all its member states. Given the large number of national jurisdictions with widely varying tax systems and rates, and the political, economic, social and technical ramifications of a common VAT system, the issue of tax harmonisation within the EU was a complex process, comparable to the complexity with our own efforts at harmonising the central and state taxes into a unified GST.

Beginning with 1967, the EU issued a series of VAT Directives over the next few years requiring the member states to adapt their domestic legislations to a common format of VAT and reached agreements with the member states on this. The idea was to promote free movement of persons, goods, services and capital across the national borders of the EU members; ensure tax neutrality within the commercial exchanges; encourage fair competition by eliminating fiscal and tax barriers; and establish a will to deal with common policies such as foreign trade, agriculture, transport, energy, regional policies and environment.[13]

To ensure the neutrality, simplicity and workability of the VAT system, common rules were framed defining the scope and base of the tax, and harmonising the regulations regarding its payment and territoriality, exemptions, deductions and reporting requirements. It also made the entire EU a level playing field for all its members. Harmonisation is always a difficult process, but a simple and uniform VAT system it creates always fosters economic efficiency of the tax system as a whole by reducing distortions and minimising compliance and collection problems. Different rates invariably cause legal and administrative quagmire and lead to classification problems as dealers and producers always tend to put the good in a lower tax slab.

---

[13] Bedri Peci and Fitore Morina, 'The Legal Framework for Harmonization of Value Added Tax (VAT) in European Union', *Juridica* 13, no. 1 (2017): 83–96.

In France, VAT is not applicable on exports or transactions relating to ships and aircraft; intra-community supplies and similar transactions; teaching; medical and paramedical services; hospital care costs; insurance and reinsurance; certain banking operations such as commitments, guarantees and other forms of security interest; the management of credit guarantees by the grantor of the credit, etc. Companies whose annual turnover does not exceed €82,800 for sales or €33,100 for service providers are exempt from paying VAT, but they often opt to pay VAT anyway because otherwise they will not be eligible to claim VAT back on their business investments. Periodicity of VAT payment depends on the turnover; businesses whose annual turnover falls between €82,800 and €788,000 for sale of goods or between €33,100 and €238,000 for service providers are required to make two tax payments in each financial year, while companies whose turnover exceeds €788,000 for goods sold or €238,000 for services rendered must pay their VAT on a monthly basis.

In France, currently there are several rates of VAT, the standard rate being 20 per cent which covers about 55 per cent of the products in the price index. There are two reduced rates: a 10 per cent rate for restaurants, transport, renovation/improvement works and certain medical drugs; and a 5.5 per cent rate for most groceries like food items, water and non-alcoholic beverages, books, special equipment for the disabled and school canteens, some entertainment events and some domestic personal services. There is also a specific rate of 2.1 per cent applicable only in relation to prescription drugs reimbursed by social security, TV licences, sale of live animals, press publications and certain entertainment events. Other VAT rates apply in overseas territories (Guadeloupe, Martinique and La Réunion) and Corsica.[14] The exempted supplies include land

---

[14] In Corsica, the rates are 20 per cent (standard) and 0.9 per cent, 2.1 per cent, 10 per cent and 13 per cent for specified goods or services. For overseas

under specific conditions, financial transactions, buildings completed for more than five years, insurance, education, health and welfare, betting and gaming, etc.

The VAT Directives[15] require all EU member states to compulsorily exempt certain goods and services from VAT such as postal services and medical and certain paramedical services, while certain other goods and services can be optionally exempted. France uses these relaxations to exempt the supply of services by authors, artists, lawyers (up to €42,000 of annual turnover) and certain other liberal professions. The standard rate of 20 per cent in France is below the average standard rate in the EU (21.6% in 2015). Currently, the standard rate applied in the EU ranges from 17 per cent (Luxembourg) to 27 per cent (Hungary), while all the neighbours of France follow a standard rate within a narrow band of 19–21 per cent.[16] Like in India, France also taxes the petroleum products separately. The *Taxe Intérieure de Consommation sur les Produits Énergétiques* (TICPE) (Consumption Tax on Domestic Energy Products) applies to petroleum products and biofuels—petrol and gasoline, electricity, natural gas, coal and coke—but unlike in India, energy products are subject to both TICPE and VAT.

Today, for the French government, VAT is an important source of state revenues, accounting for about 15 per cent of the total tax revenues (2014), though it was less than the EU average of 17.5 per cent. VAT receipts constituted 6.9 per cent

---

dependencies, apart from the standard rate of 8.5 per cent, there are reduced rates of 2.1 per cent, 1.05 per cent and 1.75 per cent for specified goods or services (Refer: *Worldwide VAT, GST and Sales Tax Guide* [E&Y, March 2017]. Available at: http://www.ey.com/Publication/vwLUAssets/Worldwide-VAT-GST-and-sales-tax-guide-2017/$FILE/Worldwide%20VAT,%20GST%20 and%20Sales%20Tax%20Guide%202017.pdf [accessed on 30 November 2017]).

[15] 2006/112/EC (Refer: Ibid).

[16] Athena Kalyva, Hans Naudts, and Savina Princen, 'The French VAT System and Revenue Efficiency' (European Economy Economic Brief 015, July 2016), 4.

of GDP in 2014, compared to about 8 per cent during the 1970s. The VAT base over which the standard rate is applicable represents about 65 per cent of the tax base, as against 81 per cent in Germany (2014).[17] Germany and France represent the two most important economies in EU, and in both, GST in the form of VAT plays a very important role.

VAT reduced rates and exemptions considered as tax expenditures by the French authorities amounted to €17.8 billion (0.8% of GDP) in 2015, much of it (around €3 billion) on account of restaurants alone. There are arguments both for and against the use of reduced rates in GST. While reduced VAT rates may be used to address distributional concerns and to mitigate the strong regressive impact of any tax on goods and services, empirical evidence does not support that abolishing reduced rates can effectively address the equity considerations. For example, a reduced VAT rate for food or energy benefit not only low-income households but also high-income households. The redistributional aspects can possibly be addressed more effectively through the social welfare system and a progressive income tax rather than through the VAT. The argument also holds for reduced VAT rates on energy products, which in addition constitute environmentally harmful subsidies and go against environmental goals. Similar considerations apply in respect of merit goods also, as high-income earners may consume merit goods more than the others and their consumption may not be dependent on VAT rates; in such cases, reduced VAT rates may prove to be costly to the government.[18]

---

[17] Ibid., 7.

[18] French VAT rates for foodstuff (5.5%) and energy products (5.5%). For some merit goods, the rates are as follows: admission to cultural events (5.5%), periodicals and books (2.1% and 5.5%), newspapers (printed—2.1%) and supply of social services (5.5% and 10%).

The Australian Experience

In Australia, GST was introduced with effect from 1 July 2000. Although the idea had existed for at least 25 years since 1975, it was always treated with a great deal of scepticism. After the Labour Party government of Bob Hawke rejected a serious CT proposal in 1985, the proposal was revived in the 1990s by Liberal Party's leader John Hewson. But after being asked by journalist Mike Willesee to explain the arithmetic of how the price of a birthday cake would be impacted by the proposed GST, it was given up on the assumption of being 'too complicated'. In that interview, to Willesee's question, 'You tell us in what you've published that the cost of cake goes down, the cost of confectionery goes up, there's icing and maybe ice cream, and then there's candles on top of it', Hewson could only say, 'To give you an accurate answer, I need to know exactly what type of cake to give a detailed answer', prompting Willesee to retort, 'If the answer to a birthday cake is so complex—you do have an overall problem with the GST, don't you?'

In 1996, the Liberals won the federal elections after promising 'never ever' to introduce a GST. The 'never ever' was over before only two years, when, under the leadership of John Howard, Liberals fought the 1998 election on the issue of introduction of a GST that would replace all existing sales taxes and apply to all goods and services. Liberals suffered a negative vote swing of 4.61 per cent in that election, but still scraped through by winning just enough seats to remain in office. The government had to seek the support of minor parties such as the Australian Democrats to garner support in the Senate to get the GST legislation through. The legislation was passed on 28 June 1999 as 'A New Tax System (Goods and Services Tax) Act 1999' (which we shall henceforth call the GST Act in this section) and came into operation on 1 July 2000, replacing the federal wholesale sales tax system. Gradually, many state and territorial government taxes, duties and levies such as banking taxes and stamp duties would also be abolished. But the scepticism did not die down, and in the 2001 federal elections, the Labour Party made its rollback a centrepiece of its electoral campaigning, with its leader Wayne Swan describing it as a 'bastard tax'. Labour lost the election 61–69 to Liberals in the 150-member House of Representatives.

GST is a consumption-based tax of 10 per cent of the price of the goods being sold or services being supplied in respect of most goods and services with a system of input credits, proceeds of which are shared with the states. In 1999, the federal government reached agreement with the state and territory governments that their duties, levies and taxes on consumption would be removed over time. The consequent Budget shortfall would be compensated by the revenue earned from GST, just like in India, and the distribution of proceeds would be decided by the Commonwealth Grants Commission, a statutory body like the Finance Commission, to achieve horizontal fiscal equalisation, a central feature of the Australian federation. Simultaneously, for greater acceptance, federally levied personal income tax and company tax were reduced to absorb the shocks emanating from the introduction of GST. State governments in Australia do not levy any sales taxes, but stamp duties are levied on a range of transactions.

Taxable supplies, as defined in Chapter 2, Division 9, of the GST Act include supply of all goods, services and transactions made for a consideration within, from and to Australia and also cover transactions related to real properties in Australia. The threshold for compulsory registration under GST is AUS$75,000 per annum, but, like in India, businesses with lesser turnovers are also allowed to register. The advantage of registration is the eligibility for claiming input tax credits, in exchange for collecting GST from the customers and paying it to the government. A registered business also has the obligation to submit quarterly returns called business activity statements. These are required to be submitted online, and the taxes are also required to be paid online.

Some transactions are outside the scope of GST, for example, gifts by people who are unregistered or have no connection with Australia. Items such as salaries, wages, fresh food and real estate are exempt from GST. Some supplies are 'GST-free',[19] implying no liability for GST on the supply, but the supplier can claim credits for GST on the purchases made, as in the case of specified exports, health, food, education, international travel and certain charitable activities.[20] Some items, for example, rental income and financial services, are 'input-taxed',[21] implying that GST is not chargeable on their supply, but there is no entitlement to an input tax credit for anything acquired or imported to make the supply.

Like in Canada or France, here also concerns were raised that GST would impact the poor much more than the rich, being a regressive tax, but the likely regressive potential was mitigated by adopting a set of measures like abolition of federal wholesale sales tax as well as some stamp duties and fuel taxes, besides effecting reductions in rates of personal income tax and state banking tax side by side with the launching of GST. But the reactions and counter-reactions were very much like what we

---

[19] As defined in Chapter 3 of the A New Tax System (Goods and Services Tax) Act, 1999, GST-free supplies include food, health, education, childcare, exports and other supplies that are for consumption outside Australia, religious services, activities of charitable institutions, etc., water and sewerage, supplies of going concerns, transport and related matters, precious metals, supplies through inwards duty-free shops, grants of land by governments, farm land, cars for use by disabled people, international mail and telecommunication supplies made under arrangements for global roaming in Australia.
[20] http://www.ird.govt.nz/yoursituation-bus/bus-aust-nz/tax-basics/comp-gst/comp-gst.html (accessed on 30 November 2017).
[21] Division 40 of Chapter 3 of the Act defines the input taxed supplies; these include financial supplies, residential rent, residential premises, precious metals, school tuckshops and canteens, fund-raising events conducted by charitable institutions, etc.

are witnessing in India today. The major concern was as usual the impact of GST on inflation. On the government's side, the Treasurer Peter Costello admitted that in the immediate aftermath of the introduction of GST, inflation might register modest increase but the effect would abate over time 'with reductions in business tax costs as the current embedded wholesale sales taxes in the production chain are eliminated and new arrangements to reduce diesel and state reduced taxes begin to feed through the system'. It was understood that GST will take time to stabilise, and its intended consequences such as reduced business costs and increased competition which would spur consumer demands and benefit the economy would flow over time, and no miracles could be expected in the short term. To address the hardships of the consumers from the immediate price rises that might follow the introduction of GST, the treasurer asserted that the 'Government has designed the package to include income tax cuts and other measures such as increased pensions and family allowances that will more than compensate consumers for the overall increase in prices'.[22]

The behaviour of business and consumers were also strikingly similar in the two countries. In the period leading to the introduction of GST, consumption rose sharply as consumers had rushed to purchase goods that they perceived would be more expensive in the post-GST period, and traders and businesses destocked and cleaned up their inventory by offering lucrative discounts, just like in India. Thus, immediately after the GST came into effect in July 2000, both consumption and economic growth declined. Inflation increased substantially, though transitorily, in the quarter ending September 2000,

---

[22] 'Extract of the Address to the Economic Society Forecasting Conference Lunch', 19 August 1999. Available at: https://web.archive.org/web/200608 20191437/ (accessed on 29 September 2017); http:/www.treasurer.gov.au/ tsr/content/speeches/1999/006.asp (accessed on 30 November 2017).

by as much as 2.8.[23] In the first fiscal quarter of 2001, the Australian economy recorded negative economic growth for the first time in more than 10 years. The opposition, exactly like in India, cried foul and charged that GST had hit the economy badly.[24] Like in India, small businesses complained of cumbersome procedures and glitches faced in submission of quarterly business activity statements to the Australian Taxation Office online as required under law; one study, in fact, estimated that costs of compliance to the new tax system amounted to 3 per cent of annual turnovers of small businesses.[25] But consumption soon returned to normal and growth picked up gradually. In each of the countries that had introduced GST, the economy had underperformed in the year of its introduction, something that we can expect in India too. One study pointed to the negative impact of GST on the real estate market, projecting a steep rise in prices of new homes by 8 per cent and a steeper fall in demand by 12 per cent, but real estate market returned to boom between 2002 and 2004 with prices and demands both soaring, especially in cities such as Sydney and Melbourne and elsewhere.[26]

Short-term inflationary impact had characterised the switchover of GST in almost every country, and governments had intervened appropriately to arrest this, sometimes adopting

---

[23] Abbas Valadkhani and Allan P. Layton, 'Quantifying the Effect of GST on Inflation in Australia's Capital Cities: An Intervention Analysis'. Queensland University of Technology, 2003. Available: https://eprints.qut.edu.au/423/1/ (accessed on 30 September 2017).

[24] *Labor Says GST Has King Hit Economy. ABC 7.30 Report.*

[25] http://www.emeraldinsight.com/doi/abs/10.1108/eb060751 (accessed on 30 November 2017).

[26] Dale Pinto, 'Background and General Economic Impact of a GST on the Real Estate Industry', *Legal Issues in Business*, 2 (2000): 11–20. Also, http://www.abs.gov.au/AUSSTATS/abs@.nsf/2f762f95845417aeca25706c00834efa/58c63d8c5ba7af 60ca 256e9e0029079a! (accessed on 30 September 2017).

extraordinary measures and policies for limiting price escalation by businesses, for example:

(i) price freeze or control (in Belgium, Netherlands and Korea); (ii) price monitoring (in Germany and Ireland); (iii) freeze on profit margins (in Netherlands and Ireland), (iv) publicity campaign (in Korea, New Zealand, and United Kingdom); (v) enactment of counter inflation laws (in United Kingdom); and (vi) reduction of other taxes and subsidy payments to essential commodities (in Denmark).[27]

When VAT was introduced in India from 1 April 2005, no such measure was adopted. As a result, either there were unexplained increases in prices or businesses refused to reduce 'the maximum retail price despite the sharp decline in the tax rates with respect to their products', as pointed out by the CAG in one of his report in 2010.[28] We ought to be more proactive this time, having learnt from the past.

One particular concern in Australia as in India was to ensure that there was no undue profiteering in the implementation phase (1 July 1999–30 June 2002) and that the benefit of reduced costs was passed on to the consumers to mitigate the immediate impact of GST on prices. There was need for a strong and effective price monitoring and control mechanism to prevent undue profiteering by businesses, and the best way to ensure that was, as always, by ensuring free and fair competition. To this end, the Australian Competition and Consumer Commission (ACCC) was charged with ensuring that price rises faced by consumers were appropriate, and was given the legal authority to impose fines up to AUS$10 million on businesses that did not adjust the prices with the new tax rates, so as to

---

[27] Sthanu R. Nair and Leena Mary Eapen, 'Price Monitoring and Control under GST: Lessons from Australia', *Economic & Political Weekly* 52, no. 25–26 (24 June 2017). Available at: http://www.epw.in/node/148983/pdf (accessed on 30 September 2017).

[28] Ibid.

safeguard the interest of the consumers. ACCC was entrusted with the responsibility to

> (i) formulate guidelines about what constitutes price exploitation; (ii) seek information from businesses to effectively monitor the price movements; (iii) issue notice to the businesses in case they indulge in price exploitation; (iv) seek penalties before the federal court for breach of price exploitation provision by businesses and individuals; (v) accept undertakings from the businesses which are enforceable in a court; (vi) investigate complaints and issues of public concern; and (vii) provide information to both businesses and public on price exploitation provisions.[29]

It defined price exploitation and set up a mechanism for information dissemination 'to inform the consumers and businesses about the price changes due to GST' by widely distributing a publication titled *Everyday Shopping Guide with the GST*. The anti-profiteering provisions of our GST Act as discussed in Chapter 1 derived some useful ideas from the GST Acts of Australia and Malaysia. Australia, in fact, applied an anti-profiteering rule a year in advance, from July 1999.

Ten years hence, GST was recognised as a resounding success in Australia that had replaced inefficient taxes that 'imposed high deadweight costs while raising little revenue'. Social acceptance of any new tax is vital for its success, and public criticisms and debates play a significant role in informing and moulding public opinion. The political risks and costs of introducing the GST are always high, but proper management of transition and follow-up can always provide insulation to the risks. As Sinclair Davidson, a professor at RMIT University and a senior fellow at the Institute of Public Affairs, wrote,

> The GST was the last great tax reform that Australia experienced. In the subsequent ten years we have become accustomed

---

[29] Ibid.

to tax cuts, not new taxes. The GST was a well-known and well understood idea that had been tried and tested at the ballot box.[30]

There were some subsequent attempts to increase the GST rates, but the rate has since remained intact at 10 per cent.

The Chinese Experience

After Mao's death and overthrow of the infamous Gang of Four, China started opening up its economy since December 1978. Under the leadership of Deng Xiaoping, it embarked on a path of reforms it called 'Socialism with Chinese characteristics', under which, during the late 1970s and early 1980s, agriculture was freed from collectivisation, country was opened to foreign investment and private businesses were permitted for the first time—though most industries were still state-controlled. Then during the late 1980s and early 1990s, industries were privatised, price controls were removed and except for the banking and the petroleum sectors, industries were opened up to investment and competition from the private sector. The result was a spectacular growth of the private sector and sustained double-digit economic growth for the country during the next two decades.

With opening up of the economy, the archaic tax system needed an overhaul. China started to implement VAT in 1984 on 24 specified taxable items. Then a major structural reform which had long become overdue was finally undertaken in 1993. On 13 December 1993, the State Council of China promulgated 'The Provisional Regulations of the People's Republic of China on Value-added Tax', which came into effect on 1 January

---

[30] Sinclair Davidson, 'Taxing Questions: 10 Years of GST'. Available at: http://www.abc.net.au/news/2010-07-01/36428 (accessed on 30 November 2017).

1994 pursuant to China's goal of 'unification of taxation management, equity of tax burden, simplification of tax system, rationalisation of revenue distribution relations and guarantee of the financial revenue'. It expanded the VAT to include the sale of most goods as well as processing, and repair services.[31]

VAT is administered by the State Administration of Taxation, revenue from which is shared between the central government (75%) and local governments (25%). It is the major source of fiscal revenue for the governments in China, particularly the central government (32% of total tax revenues in 2015). VAT is payable by all enterprises or individuals selling merchandise or engaged in processing, repairing, assembling services or importing goods within the territory of the People's Republic of China on the value added at each stage of their production, selling, repairing or other processes.

While VAT applied to most goods, China introduced and gradually expanded a business tax (BT) to include services in the tax net. Service sector, like in India, was increasing its contribution to the national GDP and in 2015, it accounted for more than half of China's GDP for the first time; it was also growing at a faster rate than any other sector of the economy. Under the BT regime, service industries were forced to pay higher taxes across supply chains while being unable to benefit from the deductions and input tax credits allowed by VAT. It was then that the next step, which indeed was a transformational step, was taken to integrate the taxes on goods and services. Following the success of a pilot project undertaken in Shanghai in 2012 before it was rolled out nationwide on 1 August 2013, most services were brought under VAT. By the end of 2015, postal, telecommunication and transportation services were covered by a nationwide VAT regime. In March 2016, the government

---

[31] Tax Policy Department, Ministry of Finance, 'Briefing of VAT under China's Tax System', 13 March 2017. Available at: http://www.china.org.cn/english/LivinginChina/202770.htm (accessed on 30 November 2017).

announced that major industries paying BT would be transitioned to the VAT regime. From 1 May 2016, coverage of VAT was extended to construction, finance, lifestyle and real estate sectors, essentially abolishing the BT regime from China's taxation system. The reform was part of China's attempts to restructure the economy 'from one driven by labour-intensive manufacturing to one that is service-oriented by easing the tax burden on service industries'.[32] Since 2016, VAT has become China's most important indirect tax source other than the CT, ushering in China's most significant tax reform in more than two decades.[33] It is expected to maintain the growth in services sector and boost consumption at a time when the Chinese economy has started showing definite signs of slowing down. As the country is hoping to move ahead and arrest the slowing growth by transforming its huge base of low-end value-added manufacturing by prodding them to move higher up the value chain, the new tax regime is expected to encourage the low-end manufacturers to upgrade their outdated technology and enhance their capabilities through investments in R&D. The latest reform has extended the benefits earlier enjoyed by the manufacturing sector to the service industries, reducing their tax burden as they would now be taxed only on the value added at each stage in the supply chain.

Taxable activities under VAT are categorised as (a) supply of services, (b) supply of intangible assets and (c) supply of real estate. Supply of any service within these three categories

---

[32] Dezan Shira & Associates, 'An Overview of China's VAT Reform', 24 February 2017. Available at: https://www.chinabusinessreview.com/an-overview-of-chinas-vat-reform/ (accessed on 30 November 2017).

[33] Other indirect taxes include customs duty, stamp duty and certain local levies such as the Urban Maintenance & Construction Tax and Education Levy, some real estate-specific taxes, motor vehicle taxes and mining specific taxes (Refer: *China: Country VAT Essentials Guide 2016*. Available at: https://assets.kpmg.com/content/dam/kpmg/cn/pdf/en/2016/09/china-country-vat-essentials-guide-2016.pdf [accessed on 30 November 2017]).

falls under the jurisdiction of VAT, unless specifically excluded. Each of these three sectors is subject to different VAT rates that range from 6 per cent to 17 per cent. Companies in the real estate and construction sectors pay 11 per cent VAT, while those in the financial sector pay only 6 per cent VAT. While most services are covered under 'supply of services', the 'supply of intangible assets' includes franchise rights, memberships and virtual products such as Internet games and domain names. Under VAT, businesses are taxed according to their turnovers, either as general taxpayers or small-scale taxpayers. Small-scale taxpayers—those collecting less than RMB500,000 in revenue—benefit from a lower VAT rate of 3 per cent, compared to the higher rate of 6–17 per cent levied on general taxpayers, depending on their industry.[34] China's VAT system has some unique features in comparison to other countries. For example, in China, VAT applies to most financial services including interest income. VAT on real estate transactions involves not only business-to-business (B2B) and business-to-consumer (B2C) transactions, but also consumer-to-consumer (C2C) transactions.[35]

Zero-rated goods include exported goods and certain exported services which are eligible for input tax credits. Agricultural products, contraceptive drugs and devices, antique books and most exported services are exempt from VAT, while interest income on deposits derived by financial institutions, claims paid by insurers and certain merger and acquisition activities are outside its scope. Foreign entities are not eligible to register as general VAT taxpayers in China.[36]

While the VAT reform has brought down the levels of taxation across the board and unified the country in terms of the system of indirect taxation, the new system has also created its

---

[34] Ibid.
[35] Ibid.
[36] Ibid.

own complexities and conundrums, and the process of adjustment for industries to the new system could be a painful one. For example, real estate, construction, finance and lifestyle services sectors constituted nearly 80 per cent of the total revenue under the BT regime. Now the real estate and construction industries are closely intertwined between themselves and with finance, since without institutional financing, they cannot function. The new regime has now introduced different rules for these allied sectors, and will impact them differently, with implications on suppliers and customers as well as on price. Developers can get a VAT input credit for purchase of the rights to land use, and therefore only need to pay taxes on the value they add to their properties. But the construction industry has fewer opportunities to claim VAT credit, since labour costs are not deductible and several raw materials, for example, sand and gravel, are not considered to involve any value addition.[37] Thus, the field is uneven for different players, and the situation has some parallels in our country too.

Further, the new VAT regime, while allowing lower VAT rates (3%) to small-scale taxpayers, discriminates against them by effectively treating the large-scale businesses preferentially. While the large businesses pay higher VAT, they are also entitled to VAT export exemptions and refunds; they are also allowed to issue special VAT invoices allowing deduction of input VAT. Given these advantages, the buyers are likely to do business with them in order to offset their own taxes. Such discrimination may further accentuate the divide between the poor and the rich and increase the inequality further in a country with an already unsustainably high level of inequality, and will work against the long-term economic interests of China.[38]

---

[37] Ibid.

[38] Dezan Shira & Associates, 'An Overview of China's VAT Reform', ed. Alexander Chipman Koty, China Briefing, 30 December 2016. Available at: http://www.

With effect from 17 July 2017, China's VAT rate structure has further been reduced from four to three tiers (6%, 11% and 17%) by reducing the tax rates on farm produce, tap water and books from 13 per cent to 11 per cent. In August 2017, China decided to carry the VAT reform further forward, and fine-tune the tax administration for securing maximum results. As the Chinese Premier Li Keqiang stated, 'The VAT reform, besides reducing the tax burden for enterprises, can also leverage institutional reforms and contribute to innovation, entrepreneurship, job creation and expansion of the industry chain'. Tax cuts are estimated to have saved businesses RMB1.61 trillion (US$241.1 billion) so far until June 2017, including RMB85.12 billion since May 2016 reforms, according to the Ministry of Finance.[39]

Besides VAT, the only other indirect tax in China is the CT, which is imposed on all individuals and organisations engaged in manufacturing, processing, importing or selling taxable products.[40] In 2015, China's CT revenue amounted to RMB890.7 billion, compared to RMB3,111 billion from VAT. The VAT revenue in 2016 was RMB4,071 billion, an increase of more than 31 per cent over 2015.[41] Even the CT is expected

---

china-briefing.com/news/2016/12/30/overview-chinas-vat-reform.html (accessed on 30 November 2017).

[39] Xu Wei, 'China to Press Ahead with Value-added Tax Reform', 18 August 2017. Available at: http://english.gov.cn/premier/news/2017/08/18/content_281475799085376.htm (accessed on 30 November 2017).

[40] CT is levied on five categories of products: (a) products whose over-consumption is harmful to health, social order and the environment, for example, tobacco, alcohol, firecrackers and fireworks; (b) luxury goods and non-necessities such as precious jewellery and cosmetics; (c) high-energy consumption and high-end products such as passenger cars and motorcycles; (d) non-renewable and non-replaceable petroleum products such as gasoline and diesel oil; and (e) financially significant products such as motor vehicle tires.

[41] China Briefing, 'A Guide to Consumption Tax in China', 27 April 2016. Available at: http://www.china-briefing.com/news/2016/04/27/guide-consumption-tax-china.html (accessed on 30 November 2017).

to be reformed in the near future to effect better synergy with the nationwide VAT regime. VAT has already transformed the Chinese economy from a largely production-based economy into a predominantly service-oriented economy, and the VAT reform integrating indirect taxes on goods and services has indeed been a path-breaking and transformational reform in the history of China's taxation system.

The Malaysian Experience

Indonesia was the first ASEAN country to implement GST in 1984. Other members soon followed suit one by one: The Philippines in 1988, Thailand in 1992, Singapore in 1994, Vietnam in 1999, Cambodia in 1999, Laos in 2009 and Malaysia in 2015. After Malaysia, India was the latest country to make the transition to GST.

Until 1 April 2015, Malaysia had no GST; it only had a sales tax and a service tax. Both were federal CTs, governed respectively by the Sales Tax Act, 1972, and the Service Tax Act, 1975. While the sales tax was imposed on a wide variety of goods, the service tax was levied on consumers of certain taxable services. Both were single-stage taxes levied at the point of supply of goods or services. The rates ranged from 5 per cent to 25 per cent, depending on items. The service tax attracted a uniform rate of 6 per cent, but the sales tax rates varied from item to item, from 5 per cent for basic foodstuff to 20 per cent for alcoholic drinks and 25 per cent for cigarettes and tobacco. The threshold for compulsory licensing was RM100,000.[42] Malaysia also imposes an excise duty on luxury and 'sin' products such as automobiles, liquor, beer and tobacco products in addition.

---

[42] Max Schofield, 'Malaysia's New GST: A Brief Comparison with its Former Sales Tax and Service Tax Regime', 24 April 2015. Available at: https://www.bna.com/malaysias-new-gst-b17179925799/ (accessed on 30 November 2017).

Because of the inadequacies of the existing structure, Malaysia has been toying with the idea of introducing a GST since 2009. The government was trying to mobilise additional revenues to offset its Budget deficits and reduce its dependence on PETRONAS, Malaysia's state-owned oil company which was a major revenue earner for the government. The GST Bill, 2009, was tabled for its first reading at the Dewan Rakyat, the Lower House of the Malaysian Parliament, on 16 December 2009.[43] It attracted mounting criticism from the public and the opposition parties, and proved to be extremely unpopular for fear of its adverse effect on the low-income Malaysians. The government finally had to put off its implementation. The new tax was expected to increase revenue by RM1 billion from RM12 billion garnered from the current sales tax scheme at that time. Perhaps enough awareness was not created about its benefits which include lower business costs, improved accounting and reduced evasion and tax frauds.[44]

It is always challenging to introduce any new system, especially in regard to taxation as it impacts individuals, businesses, government and economy as a whole, and there is need to establish an appropriate regulatory mechanism to strike a judicious balance between the interests of all stakeholders as well as between the benefits and disadvantages of the new system. The opposition to GST arose not only from considerations of the inflationary potential of the new tax leading to possible increases in the prices of most goods, or from the fact that

---

[43] Lee Yuk Peng, 'Parliament: GST Bill Tabled for First Reading (Update)', The Star Online, 16 December 2009. Available at: https://web.archive.org/web/20110621235452/; http:/thestar.com.my/news/story.asp?-file=%2F2009%2F12%2F16%2Fnation%2F20091216102228&sec=nation (accessed on 30 November 2017).

[44] 'Government Defends GST Delay, Scoffs at PR's Victory Claims', Malaysian Insider, 15 March 2010. https://web.archive.org/web/20100322190557/; http://www.themalaysianinsider.com/index.php/malaysia/56278 (accessed on 29 September 2017).

many non-tax-paying citizens would now have to bear the tax burden on account of the new GST, but also from the technological challenges that it posed to businesses, especially small businesses, which were mostly unaccustomed to the computer and GST software they were now forced to handle. A case was reported from Teluk Intan where a hardware store owner, Chen, 65, attempted to commit suicide in frustration from the pressure and inability to understand and implement the GST in his own business.[45]

After initially putting of the implementation until the third quarter of 2011, the government had to postpone it for a long time. The GST Act was again introduced in the Parliament on 31 March 2014 and was promulgated in June 2014 after receiving the Royal assent. Finally, on 1 April 2015, a uniform 6 per cent GST was launched, replacing the sales-and-service tax regime of indirect taxes, to be administered by the Royal Malaysian Customs Department. The effect was disruptive; inflation went up immediately, consumer confidence nosedived and public protests against the tax erupted. But the timing of its implementation had coincided with the steep global slump in oil and gas prices between 2014 and 2016, and the successful implementation of the GST had helped the federal treasury to cushion the impact of lower oil revenues; by that time, the public protests and opposition had also fizzled out. Twelve months later, business confidence was restored and 70 per cent of the businesses surveyed reported growth. As the Malaysian prime minister had rightly said, 'GST has been our saviour'.[46]

Like in India, Malaysia also had a problem of black economy, with estimates of it ranging from 9 per cent to 27 per cent

[45] 'Man Driven to Suicide Attempt over GST Woes', 11 May 2015. Available at: http://www.malaysiandigest.com/news/553188-man-driven-to-suicide-attempt-over-gst-woes.html (accessed on 30 November 2017).

[46] Jeyapalan Kasipillai and Rick Krever, 'Malaysia's GST Journey: Past, Present and Future'. Paper presented at the VAT Symposium at Pretoria, South Africa, 19 and 20 October 2016.

of GDP, and emphasising the need for a more efficient and effective tax enforcement regime. The World Bank has reported that the 'hidden or informal economy' constitutes 31 per cent of the Malaysian economy, almost double the percentage in other Asian countries such as Vietnam (15.6%) and Singapore (13%). Just like in India in the post-demonetisation period, the Malaysian post-GST implementation phase had seen many seizures and confiscation of goods such as liquor, cigarettes, tyres and controlled items[47] such as rice and sugar of huge values. To tap the lost revenues from such activities was one of the objectives behind the introduction of GST.[48]

The Malaysian GST is a federal CT with a broad base, payable by intermediaries on all stages of the supply chain on the value added, and with the final tax burden ultimately borne by the consumer as everywhere else, with input credits available at each link in the supply chain, to be offset at the subsequent stages—thus converting the single-stage sales and service taxes to a multi-stage single CT. The procedural changes that it necessitated were phenomenal, from requirements of registration and invoicing to penalty and interest rates, and it shook up the entire gamut of commercial operations in Malaysia. At the end of June 2016, there were over 7,294 GST appeal cases, indicating the extent of taxpayer grievances.

The mandatory registration threshold for the new tax is RM500,000 of annual taxable turnover. There are no reduced rates, but several exemptions (zero-rated supplies) are allowed, which include agricultural products, essential foodstuff, livestock and poultry products, fish, first 300 kwh of electricity for domestic use, water for domestic users, goods supplied to the designated areas of Labuan, Langkawi and Tioman, exports, some selected services, petrol, diesel and LPG, sale

---

[47] In Malaysia, most essential daily food consumables are controlled items and the ceiling price is set by the government.
[48] Kasipillai and Krever, 'Malaysia's GST Journey'.

of residential properties and non-commercial public services. The law mandates that all prices must be quoted inclusive of GST and the GST component must be shown separately.

As of May 2016, 412,715 entities including 229,319 companies (55.6%) had registered for GST. A GST-audit carried out by Customs officials found that the group that comprises sole proprietors, partnerships or individuals was the least compliant among all groups; they constituted 41 per cent of the total registered entities.[49]

Administration of a complex tax like GST is a problem anywhere, and Malaysia has been no exception in this. While implementing a tax like this without generating large-scale turbulence in the economy, it is essential that a suitable scheme for compensation and mitigation of unintended consequences, especially on small businesses which are unequipped to deal with such disruptions, be carefully worked out and a comprehensive awareness campaign be launched simultaneously to inform the public about the benefits and implications of the new system, and to help them comply with the technical requirements, especially those associated with mandatory filing of returns.

In fact, following the introduction of GST, the government had created a social safety net in the form of monetary assistance to compensate poor households, along with a package of measures to mitigate the impact of the new tax. In the 2016 Budget, RM5.9 billion were allocated to a Malaysia People's Assistance scheme to benefit about 4.7 million households and 2.7 million single individuals, to address the adverse distributional effect of GST. But the concerns of the SMEs were not properly addressed; about one-third of the firms audited by the Malaysian Customs during September 2016 were facing problems, especially in relation to provide correct information in

---

[49] Ibid.

their GST returns. In particular, a study found that the adverse impact of GST on small businesses was not gauged correctly, suggesting that

> The government should critically assess the magnitude and social impact of closure of small traditional businesses which resulted from their inability to cope with GST regulations. In addition, a more sympathetic approach should be devised to support this alienated group of small traders so that they could continue to make a living in the new tax regime.[50]

There also remains the problem of psychological and corruption costs eroding the tax base, and creating a gap between potential and actual revenue realised from GST; unless properly monitored, this gap has the potential to widen.[51]

There is also the need to create a wider consultative mechanism involving all players and stakeholders. In Malaysia, a GST Technical Committee comprising professional bodies and trade chambers exists to address all technical issues through quarterly meetings, but without a representative from the Ministry of Finance, it is perceived to be ineffective.[52] In India, the GST Council which is entirely constituted by the finance ministers performs a similar function. But in both countries, a formal and institutional consultative mechanism is absent that takes on board the views of external stakeholders such as industry associations, government agencies and professional bodies who are potentially impacted by policies and procedures relating to the new tax. Such a wider mechanism can create its own dynamics to detect and arrest errors and glitches and offset possible resentment or grievances of some stakeholders.

On an annualised basis, GST contributed about 18 per cent to Malaysia's federal revenue in 2015, a share that is bound to

---

[50] Ibid.
[51] Ibid.
[52] Ibid.

increase substantially with an expanding economy. Share of GST varies widely from country to country depending upon the structure of their tax systems and expenditure priorities, and the rates as well as threshold amounts also show wide variations. Thus, no horizontal comparison among different countries in respect of GST will be valid. About 160 countries have adopted some form of VAT or GST, but most of these would be vastly different from the dual destination-based system that Canada and India are following. Among the OECD countries most of which had switched over to VAT/GST during the 1970s and 1980s, Chile raises as much as 55 per cent of its total tax revenue from GST, followed by Turkey (44%) and Mexico (36%), while Japan raises only 20 per cent of its total revenue from GST, as against the OECD average of 33 per cent.[53]

As regards the rate, it varies from 5 per cent in Canada to 6 per cent in Malaysia, 15 per cent in New Zealand, 19 per cent in Germany, 20 per cent in France and 27 per cent in Hungary. Many countries have subsequently increased the tax rates. Japan had introduced a CT in 1989, the rate of which was increased from 3 per cent to 5 per cent in 1997. The effect was devastating; Japan went into recession, but GST might not have been the only reason. In 2013, the Shinzo Abe government increased it to 8 per cent, while postponing further proposed increase to 10 per cent until October 2019. The Malaysian government had given the assurance of keeping the rate unchanged during 2017. Singapore had introduced GST in 1994 at a low rate of 3 per cent with a high threshold limit of SGD1 million, but the rate has been increased thrice since 2003 to 7 per cent in 2007. New Zealand implemented GST in 1985 and the rate has been increased twice to the current level of 15 per cent in 2010.[54]

---

[53] 2015 figures, OECD Revenue Statistics 2016. Available at: http://www.oecd.org/tax/tax-policy/revenue-statistics.htm (accessed on 30 November 2017).

[54] *Worldwide VAT, GST and Sales Tax Guide 2017.*

Summing Up

The discussion on the GST experiences spanning several countries makes one thing clear—that GST everywhere has followed more or less the same track and run the same course, causing similar ripples, disruptions and turbulence, but everywhere these distortions have proved to be transitory. Ultimately, the new system has found its own equilibrium in every country wherever it was launched, and there is no instance of any country rolling back the new system after having launched it. Everywhere, there were initial spikes in inflation, and economic growth took a beating in the immediate aftermath of the launch of the GST, partly due to the destocking and excess consumption just before its launch and a slump in demand and the consequent underperformance of the economy afterwards. But eventually, growth had picked greater momentum than before and inflation could be controlled everywhere.

As per the latest forecasts made by the IMF in October 2017, India's GDP growth for 2017 will slow down to 6.7 per cent from its earlier estimate of 7.2 per cent, due to the lingering impact of demonetisation and transition to GST, but it will bounce back to 7.4 per cent in the next year, making India the fastest-growing major economy again, higher than China's 6.5 per cent. The IMF also expects the Indian economy to grow 8 per cent in the medium term on the back of reforms undertaken so far. This fits the story we have narrated earlier.

The Indian experience is, thus, a repeat of this universal trend, and there is no particular reason for despondency at the developments that we are witnessing again; these are undesirable but not unexpected outcomes, if we are to relate to the experiences of other countries in our globally connected world, because behaviour of the consumer and businesses remains identical everywhere. The transition phase we are passing through could be longer and more difficult than we might hope, especially in a complex and diverse country like India. It is crucial that this transitional phase be carefully negotiated, by drawing lessons from some of the countries discussed earlier. As these experience show without exception, GST delivers in the long run, and by long run, we reckon a time horizon of three–five years. In the end, GST has been working well in every country.

Global experiences also tell us that our GST design may not be as imperfect as it is made out to be by its critics. In many countries, there are multiples rates and a wide variety of exempted goods and services, and essential supplies needed by the poor often attract a reduced rate. Real estate and petroleum are covered in some countries but excluded in some others. There cannot be a one-size-fits-all kind of a solution; different countries have different systems coexisting and functioning optimally at the national and subnational levels, as in Canada. A country needs to experiment in the context of its own problems and situations, and then discover the solution that suits its own realities.

SMEs have been impacted negatively almost everywhere; they need to be supported, and their genuine concerns about lack of capacity and technological weaknesses need to be addressed. Awareness and public education are essential for success of any new system to make way for its acceptance and voluntary compliance, without which no tax system can ever achieve its objectives. There are many lessons to be learnt from the international experiences and the sooner we learn them, the better it would equip us to avoid the pitfalls, for other countries have faced similar pitfalls and learnt from them. Each country that experimented with GST had to negotiate a difficult transition, and if we can learn a thing or two from their mistakes; we shall not only be wiser but be better equipped to manage our own transition which, certainly, is not going to be easy. But, as the Urdu poet Jigar Moradabadi wrote,

Jo tufanon men palte ja rahe hain

Vahi duniya badalte ja rahe hain.

(Only he who negotiates his way through the tempest of life can transform it.)

Chapter Four

Overcoming Hurdles and Challenges

Challenges Galore

On 9 October 2017, over 90 lakh truckers went on a two-day nationwide chakka jam to protest against various issues ranging from disruptive impact of GST and the continued extortion by transport officials at the Regional Transport Office (RTO) barriers in many states, causing loss of over ₹4,000 crore to the road transport sector. The truckers also demanded that since diesel, along with toll, accounts for more than 70 per cent of their cost of operations, diesel prices must be slashed and diesel be brought under the GST regime. Before that, in July itself just after the new tax regime was launched, textile workers had gone on strike from Gujarat and Tamil Nadu against the 5 per cent tax imposed on textiles, followed by strikes by traders in Kerala against the rise in prices of various commodities as a result of what they had called 'faulty' GST implementation. These strikes and protests were only to be expected because as we have observed, GST is a disruptive and transformational reform, and disruption often leads to disorder as businesses take time to adjust to a new tax regime, and those that cannot often perish. It is the price and the downside for any transformational reform.

Apart from the informal sector that was already reeling under the severe blow from last year's demonetisation, the export sector was also badly affected by the implementation of GST. There were many other challenges as well, like those emanating from an inefficient GSTN that could not handle the massive transaction processing it was supposed to handle, affecting all taxpayers. There were problems related to the filing of returns faced by taxpayers due to their unfamiliarity with the software systems, and other technical problems. Small businesses and manufacturing SMEs in particular are at the receiving end and facing a higher tax burden. Under the previously extant excise laws, only those manufacturers whose turnover exceeded ₹1.50 crore were liable to pay excise duty. But under GST now, the turnover threshold has been reduced to only ₹20 lakh, and many of the manufacturers who were outside the tax net under the earlier tax regime have now become taxpayers. Seeding of PAN in the GST registration and the electronic processing of entire transactions have now made it virtually impossible for businesses to evade taxes, and the manufacturing SMEs have to now bear the tax burden if they are to claim the benefits of input credits. In case of SMEs with a turnover of up to ₹75 lakh, even though they can opt for the composition scheme and pay only 1 per cent tax on turnover in lieu of GST and hence reduce their compliance costs, they are not eligible to claim any input tax credit, and the choice would be a difficult one.

The informal sector in particular will suffer the worst, but it may nudge them to move into the formal stream. As a commentator wrote in the *Economic Times*, 'GST will put paid to India's informal sector, drawing most of it into the formal universe and killing off much of what is left behind. This change will erode the flexibility the economy derives from informality and has serious implications for India's political economy'.[1] The informal sector, largely comprising thousands of small, ancillary industrial units, employing very few employees, plays an integral part in the supply chain of production for our manufacturing businesses. They function with minimal over-heads, are forced to accept delayed payment for their supplies while making prompt payment to their own suppliers and are always struggling for working capital. Most of these, without easy access to bank credits, are forced to borrow from private sources at atrociously high interest rates.

There are no reliable studies on the informal sector or assessment of their contribution to the economy, but most agree that the informal sector employs almost 90 per cent of India's labour force. Large companies, in manufacturing and other sectors, outsource much of their work to the informal sector, to cut their costs; even in the government sector, most housekeeping and security jobs are now being contracted out to this sector. While large entities carry the legal obligation to pay minimum wages and provident fund, health, social security and other benefits to their direct employees, they can reduce the costs of such obligation by sourcing a part of their supplies from the ancillary units that do not, and cannot, discharge any such obligation. Contract workers are, therefore, increasingly replacing the direct workers in all companies, and the condition or possible exploitation of such workers are never brought under the spotlight. They are paid a pittance, enjoy no rights or privileges as employees and the employer has no obligation towards them in the event of their dismissal. The social consequence of such subcontracting rarely attracts the attention that it deserves, except in the event of some 'newsworthy' calamity. For the government sector, even though the workers are

[1] T. K. Arun, 'A Defining Feature of India's Economy Has Just Fallen Prey to the Beauty of GST', *The Economic Times*, 20 September 2017.

ultimately paid by the public exchequer, there is no guarantee at all about the fairness of their recruitment process or assurance against exploitation by their employers, unlike in every other government employment.

Under the GST regime, any firm, in order to be able to claim the input tax credit, must procure its supplies only from the dealers registered with the GSTN. Once registered, they will have to file returns and upload invoices, failing which no business is likely to buy from them, because the invoice will be needed by the buyer to ascertain the GST paid on the supplied items which the buyer will be able to claim as input tax credit—this is the GST's 'in-built incentive to comply'. But once registered, all transaction details including sales and input purchases and hence income will be automatically accessible to the tax departments, including the income tax authorities, making it impossible to evade taxes. Tax authorities will not consider their difficulties and constraints, like the high interest costs (even though this can be claimed as deduction from taxable income) or lack of working capital; the extra tax burden they will have to bear will eat into their narrow profit margins, threatening the survival of many of them. The trail of their transactions will, of course, lead the tax authorities to the lender of their loans, the suppliers of their inputs and buyers of their outputs. Thus, the informal sector will be phased out gradually—and in the process thousands of the small ancillary units of today might cease to exist. The demonetisation was meant to push these units into the formal sector by mopping up the cash from the market on which they survived, and in the process driving many of these entities out of business. GST now offers them only two choices, either to join the formal stream or close their businesses. Many 'owners' or proprietors of such concerns may eventually have to join the workforce as casual or wage labourers. Reform is never painless, but it is always more painful for those at the bottom of the economic pyramid.

The process is irreversible and in the end will be beneficial to all businesses including the small ones, but not all the entities will survive to take advantage of those benefits when they start accruing for everyone. In this sense, GST is more a business reform than a tax reform measure.

Benefits vis-à-vis Costs

About the benefits of GST, there is universal agreement that GST has the potential to create an unfragmented, unified market throughout the country, eliminate cascading of taxes, remove entry barriers and make movement of goods and services free throughout the country. It will reduce the transaction costs of business and, by matching input tax credits in successive stages of the value chain, create interlocking incentives for compliance between the supplier and the buyer, and make the evasion of taxes virtually impossible for businesses. An additional benefit will be the increase in revenue productivity of income tax, as the Income Tax Department will be able to access an individual dealer's transactions by virtue of PAN details compulsorily to be provided by a dealer during the process of GST registration. All these could contribute to acceleration in the country's economic growth. GST indeed has the potential to turn a non-tax-compliant society like ours into a reasonably tax-compliant society, thereby pushing a substantial part of the black economy into the formal stream. The question is about the associated costs and the time taken for such transformation. About its long-term benefits, there are no doubts; it is only the short-term obstacles that need to be addressed, and addressed as quickly as possible to mitigate the adverse effects which are sure to follow otherwise, which, if not managed well, may not only lead to the loss of the intended benefits and the momentum of implementation but also have a debilitating impact on inflation and economic growth. Some signs of these are already visible, though these are not worrying enough as yet.

Any tax reform will have to take into consideration the usual costs associated with any taxation system: costs of compliance, administration and distortion. Cost of compliance of GST will vary from sector to sector and on the nature and scale of businesses. Compliance cost includes the cost of preparation and filing of returns, online payment of tax and claiming of input credits. For the service sector, the cost is likely to go up substantially, as service providers need to be registered in every state where they are providing services and file returns for each registration; so far they needed to be registered only with the Centre. The number of returns will thus go up from only 2 at present to as many as 37, considering GSTR-1, GSTR-2 and GSTR-3 as separate returns, though some information in these returns will be pre-filled by the GST application software. In addition, they will now be subject to dual control by the Centre as well the states. For large manufacturers, the compliance cost will probably go down, as in place of monthly returns in respect of excise duty, VAT and CST, they will now be required to file only a single consolidated return. Micro, small and medium enterprises (MSMEs) will feel the pinch the hardest. Not only has their threshold been substantially reduced, but they cannot even opt for the compounding scheme which requires only a quarterly filing of returns if they are to claim the input tax credit. Traders again have to register themselves in every state where they operate, and their compliance costs will also go up substantially, especially for the small traders, for whom the cost of joining the credit chain may outweigh the benefits and may not justify the additional burden of compliance in terms of costs. The burgeoning e-commerce in the country will especially be affected, as they will now have their taxes deducted at source; they are also not eligible for the composition scheme with lesser compliance burden. E-marketplaces are now required to collect GST at source.[2] The

---

[2] This has now been deferred to April 2018.

most problematic would, of course, be the matching of input tax credits paid by the supplier and claimed by the buyer, given the humongous volume, but this as expected will get streamlined over a period as they learn from mistakes and become wiser with experience.[3]

Both filing and payment of taxes have to be online, and small businesses with grossly inadequate computer infrastructure and inadequate capacity to handle the software system will find their costs increasing manifolds. They will necessarily have to employ tax consultants and accounting professionals and incur the associated costs. In course of time, they will have to make investments in creating their own IT and enterprise resource planning (ERP) infrastructure.

The cost of administration will also likely increase in the short term, though this will even out in the longer term. Multiple rates always lead to classification disputes, many of which will lead to protracted litigation, and as Mr Govinda Rao points out, 'Having multiple rates is a sure invitation for lobbying. This also puts additional burden on administration, increases the compliance cost and the load-bearing capacity of technology needed for providing input tax credit with multiple rates by matching every invoice'. He cautioned, 'Above all, there is a palpable fear of the unknown, given the recent disruptive experience with demonetisation. Indeed, any major tax reform could lead to disruption, and the complexity of the structure and the untested technology platform adds to the fear'.[4] As the finance minister had said, there would be short-term pains for long-term gains, and one can only hope that the pains remain limited to the short term only.

Change always leads to added cost and fear of uncertainty, both of which increase with complexity of the replacement

---

[3] http://www.gstindia.com/gst-compliance-a-costly-affair/ (accessed on 16 October 2017).
[4] M. Govinda Rao, 'Entering the Age of GST', *The Hindu*, 1 July 2017.

system. Complexity of any tax structure has multiple facets—technical, structural as well as operational. A crucial part of the administrative and compliance costs of GST will concern the technological backbone of the new tax regime, the GSTN. As already stated, the GSTN is a non-profit, non-government company in which the Centre, states and some private banks and financial institutions are the stakeholders, but it will operate through multiple agencies whose services would not be free to the taxpayer for providing government-to-business (G2B) services. The GSTN will develop the IT infrastructure of the 'GST system' and provide the application programme interface (API) through which taxpayers will interact with the government for registration, uploading of invoices, filing of returns and other purposes. This will constitute what in computer parlance is known as the 'front-end' interface of the system, while the back-end interface will enable interactions between the GST system and tax authorities in the central and state governments including CBEC for approval of registration, scrutiny of returns and assessment of taxes, refunds of credits, etc.

All payments, uploading of invoices and filing of returns will have to be done electronically by all taxpayers only through the GST portal. Access to and use of technology is, therefore, crucial for all taxpayers registered with the GSTN, without which they cannot conduct business. But recognising that many taxpayers—especially those belonging to the MSMEs—may have no access to improved IT infrastructure necessary for billing, accounting, inventory management, invoicing, etc. or may not have any familiarity with IT system at all, the GSTN has created an ecosystem (Figure 4.1) of service providers who are called GST Suvidha Providers (GSPs) for providing innovative solutions (portal, mobile app, enriched API) who will act as enablers for the taxpayers to comply with the provisions of the GST law through its web portal. GSPs will play a very important role in making the GST roll-out smooth and convenient for taxpayers, and in bridging the gap between the taxpayer's

Figure 4.1: GSP Eco-System

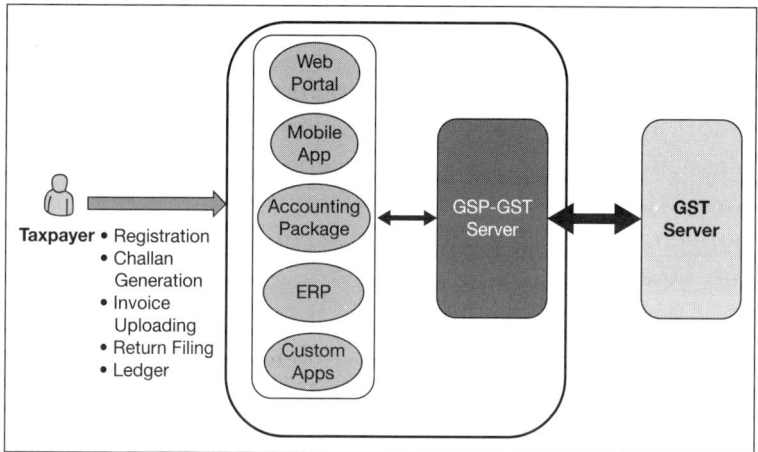

Source: http://www.gstn.org/ecosystem/ (accessed on 28 November 2017).

IT systems and the GST system. Thirty-four companies have been identified and notified as GSPs in December 2016, which include accounting software companies, ERP solution providers, IT companies, the big four accounting firms and certain other companies providing accounting and billing solutions.

To give an idea about the complexity involved in the process, just consider this: Under GST, the buyer's returns will be auto-populated by data from the seller's returns and invoices uploaded by him. The software will have to match the data automatically from the returns and uploaded invoices and accept/reject/modify these invoices. The GST system does not allow duplicate invoice upload. Synchronisation between the taxpayer's IT system and GST system will pose further challenges, and all these challenges will add to the cost of administration and compliance, as GSPs will charge the taxpayers for their services.[5]

[5] http://www.gstn.org/ecosystem/pdf/GSP_Implementation_Framework_V_3.0.pdf (accessed on 16 October 2017).

Finally, we come to the cost of distortion, which is minimised when the tax system is uniform and there are no exclusions. Prices become tax-distorted when because of the taxes, they fail to reflect the true costs and benefits. Almost all taxes distort incentives, make people to alter behaviour and lead to a less efficient allocation of the economy's resources and consequent loss of revenue. The distortion effect of taxes becomes more pronounced in the presence of inflation which effectively raises the tax burden.

A flawless GST may be a mirage, but any efficient tax reform must reduce the administration, compliance and distortion costs to the economy. An efficient tax should have a broad base and low rates with little differentiation between them, and it should be simple to administer and transparent. But with multiple rates and multiple exemptions, the present structure of GST may increase the distortions rather than moving towards neutrality, besides increasing complexities in administration and compliance. It may also lead to tax evasion and generation of black money unless these distortions are addressed properly. We have already flagged the problems likely to emanate from multiple rates leading to classification disputes, which adds to the cost of distortion.

As already noted, and as the finance minister had observed,

> The one sector in India where maximum amount of tax evasion and cash generation takes place and which is still outside the GST is real estate. Some of the states have been pressing for it. I believe that there is a strong case to bring real estate into the GST.[6]

---

[6] *The Times of India*, 'Government to Discuss Bringing Real Estate under GST in November: Arun Jaitley', *The Times of India*, 12 October 2017. Available at: https://timesofindia.indiatimes.com/business/india-business/government-to-discuss-bringing-real-estate-under-gst-in-november-arun-jaitley/articleshow/61051029.cms (accessed on 13 December 2017).

Real estate is one of the worst sectors as far as tax evasion is concerned, but the government is now showing some sensitivity to this problem. The GST Council, at its November meeting in Guwahati, is likely to consider bringing the sector under the new GST regime. Currently, GST is levied at 12 per cent on construction of a complex, building or civil structure intended for sale, wholly or partly, but land and other immovable property stand exempted from GST. If real estate is brought under GST, the final tax on the real estate sector would be almost negligible.[7]

From global experiences, it is seen that after introduction of every tax reform, consumer prices generally tend to remain high for a longer period since tax increases are passed on faster than the tax cuts. The possibility also remains that tax cuts may not be passed on to the consumer by businesses, which will fuel inflationary pressures. Following the examples of Australia and Malaysia, Indian GST has introduced anti-profiteering clauses into the GST law as discussed earlier, which will not only add to the administrative costs but may also lead to some sort of tax terrorism unless safeguards are put in place. The catch is to make the cost of evasion so exorbitant compared to the cost of compliance that taxpayers find it more beneficial to comply rather than evade taxes, and most taxpayers should find it advantageous to be within the GST system rather than outside it. Only then will it induce a behavioural change in the potential evaders.

Impact on Growth and Inflation

On 31 August 2017, the Central Statistical Organisation (CSO) released GDP data pertaining to the first quarter of the current

---

[7] http://www.business-standard.com/article/economy-policy/real-estate-might-soon-be-under-gst-arun-jaitley-117101201270_1.html (accessed on 17 October 2017).

fiscal, April–June 2017. It showed the growth in GDP during the quarter (at 2011–12 price levels) falling to only 5.7 per cent (9.3% at current market prices), the lowest recorded in the last three years, from 6.1 per cent reported during the previous quarter.[8] The left-leaning liberal economists lost no time in joining the political opposition to paint a bleak picture of imminent collapse of the Indian economy; even some BJP veterans agreed with them. It was as if a pall of universal gloom had descended over the economic future of the country, from which there was no reprieve. Every time anything has been going wrong in the country, the ghost of demonetisation is invariably blamed; it was again invoked to explain the decline in growth due to slump in demand. Now the disruption caused by GST provided another ready handle to the prophets of doom which will continue to be blamed along with demonetisation for a long time still for everything—from unemployment to loss of growth—that may cast any doubt on the health of the Indian economy. But the decline of growth during the first quarter of the current fiscal only confirmed the continuing downward trend witnessed since the last quarter of 2015–16, much before demonetisation was unleashed. GST was also launched only in the second quarter, though it also would have played a part in the subdued growth.

To be fair, both demonetisation and GST would surely have played a role in the decline in growth during the first quarter. It is also undeniable that demonetisation had desiccated consumer demands by mopping up cash temporarily from the market, and destocking by firms before the launch of GST would also have led to loss of production, even though consumer demand would temporarily rise as a result of destocking.

---

[8] Quarterly growth rates are calculated with reference not to the previous quarter but to the same quarter a year ago. GDP during Q1 of 2016–17 and 2017–18 were ₹2,941,846 crore and ₹3,110,145 crore, respectively, a rise by 5.7 per cent.

In fact, the slowdown of growth was not unexpected from these causes, but these are not the sole villains. Behind the economic downturn was a steady deterioration in the external sector combined with weakened domestic demand as well as many other factors. Export growth had declined from 10.3 per cent in the last quarter of 2016–17 to a paltry 1.2 per cent in the first quarter of 2017–18, while imports grew from 11.9 per cent to 13.4 per cent during the same period (Table 4.1). Consequently, the share of net exports (exports minus imports) in GDP had declined from (–)0.02 per cent to (–)3.27 per cent during this period; the higher negative contribution of net exports undoubtedly played a large part in the fall in growth. A strong rupee surely contributed to the depressed exports growth, but since about 60 per cent of the exports are finished goods, derived mostly from value addition on imported raw materials and inputs, devaluing the rupee would have hit the import bills and would serve no purpose. Banking sector, especially the public sector banks (PSBs) reeling under unmanageable non-performing assets (NPAs) and facing declining credit growth, was underperforming and this also contributed to the fall in GDP growth.

As is said, the devil lies in the details. It is to be remembered that our GDP is primarily consumption driven, and consumption accounts for more than two-thirds of the GDP (54% private consumption and 12.6% government consumption during 2016–17).[9] Private consumption growth has been slowing down steadily since the June 2016 quarter when its growth was 9.3 per cent, except for an astonishing spike during the demonetisation period. In the quarter ended June 2017, its growth had fallen to only 6.7 per cent. There could be several reasons for this other than the post-demonetisation cash crunch

---

[9] Statement 2, Press Note on Estimates of Gross Domestic Product for the First Quarter (April–June) of 2017–18, Ministry of Statistics & Programme Implementation, Government of India.

Table 4.1: Movement of the Growth Rates of Selected Economic Indicators: March 2016–June 2017

Indicators	Growth (Y-0-Y %) for Quarter Ending (At Constant 2011–12 Prices)					
	March 2016	June 2016	September 2016	December 2016	March 2017	June 2017
GDP	9.1	7.9	7.5	7.0	6.1	5.7
GVA[a]	8.7	7.6	6.8	6.7	5.6	5.6
GVA: Agriculture	1.5	2.5	4.1	6.9	5.2	2.3
GVA: Industry	10.3	7.4	5.9	6.2	3.1	1.6
GVA: Services	10.0	9.0	7.8	6.9	7.2	8.7
Private Final Consumption Expenditure (PFCE)[b]	9.3	8.4	7.9	11.1	7.3	6.7
Government Final Consumption Expenditure (GFCE)[c]	4.1	16.6	16.5	21.0	31.9	17.2
Gross Fixed Capital Formation (GFCF)[d]	8.3	7.4	3.0	1.7	-2.1	1.6
Core GVA[e]	10.7	8.4	6.7	5.9	3.8	5.5
Exports	-2.3	2.0	1.5	4.0	10.3	1.2
Imports	-4.3	-0.5	-3.8	2.1	11.9	13.4
Net Exports as % of GDP	0	-0.9	-0.8	-0.7	-0.3	-3.2
Index of Industrial Production (%)	5.5	8.9	5.7	2.6	2.7	-0.2
CPI Inflation	4.83	5.77	4.39	3.41	3.81	1.54

FDI (US$ Billion)	10.6	7.6	14.0	14.2	7.6	10.4
BoP (US$ Billion)	-0.3	-0.4	-3.5	-8.0	-3.4	-14.3
Trade Balance (₹ Crore)	-652	-25,702	-23,572	-22,817	-10,582	-101,668

Sources: National accounts data: Ministry of Statistics and Programme Implementation, 'Quarterly Estimates of GDP at Constant Prices, 2011–12 Series'. Available at: http://mospi.nic.in/data (accessed on 28 November 2017); FDI data: Department of Industrial Policy and Promotion. Available at: http://dipp.nic.in (accessed on 28 November 2017); IIP Data: http://www.mospi.gov.in/sites/default/files/press_release/iip_PR_12may17.pdf (accessed on 28 November 2017); External balances data: https://rbi.org.in (accessed on 28 November 2017).

Notes: Quarter ended December 2017 includes the demonetisation period.

[a]GDP is the sum of private consumption, gross investment in the economy, government investment, government spending and net foreign trade (difference between exports and imports), and has traditionally been used to measure the output of an economy. However, economists now prefer to use the concept of GVA as a useful measure of output. It provides the rupee value for the amount of goods and services produced in an economy after deducting the cost of inputs and raw materials that have gone into the production of those goods and services. The two are related by GDP = GVA + Taxes − Subsidies (on those goods and services).

[b]The PFCE is defined as the expenditure incurred on final consumption of goods and services by the resident households and non-profit institutions serving households (NPISHs).

[c]General GFCE includes all government current expenditures for purchases of non-durable goods and services net of sales and expenditure on compensation of employees as well as consumption of fixed capital (depreciation). By convention, expenditure on durable goods, which are used for defence, are also treated as part of consumption expenditure of the government.

[d]GFCF refers to the net increase in physical assets (investment minus disposals) within the measurement period (usually one year). It does not account for the consumption (depreciation) of fixed capital, and also does not include land purchases.

[e]Core GVA as defined here is the aggregate of mining, manufacturing, utilities, construction, domestic trade and transport, and finance, real estate and related services.

Figure 4.2

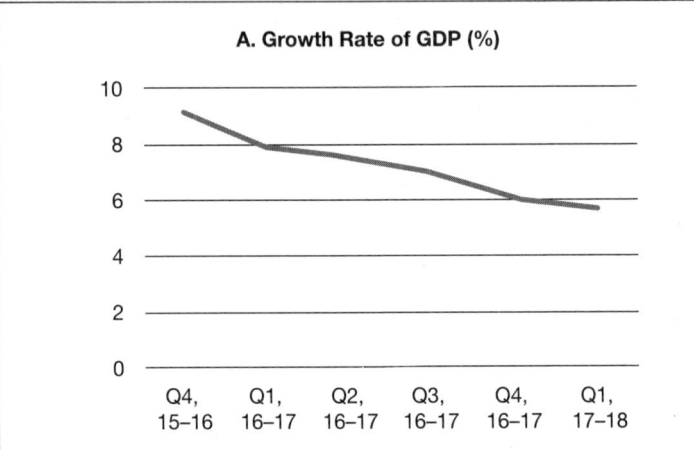

A. Growth Rate of GDP (%)

A. Growth rate of GDP has been falling continuously since the fourth quarter of 2015–16.

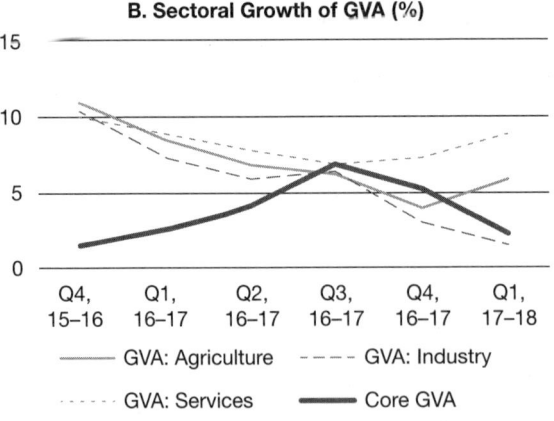

B. Sectoral Growth of GVA (%)

B. While the GVA in industry and agriculture continue with their falling trend of growth, the core GVA and GVA in service sector are showing healthy signs of growth.

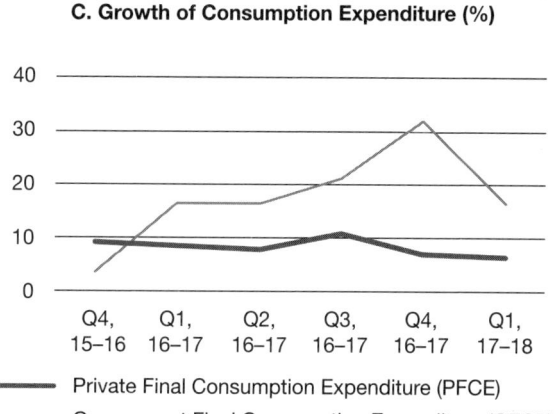

C. Growth of Consumption Expenditure (%)

— Private Final Consumption Expenditure (PFCE)
— Government Final Consumption Expenditure (GFCE)

C. The fall in private consumption since the third quarter of 2016–17 (which includes the demonetisation period) has been more than compensated by a jump in government consumption during this quarter to offset the effect of demonetisation.

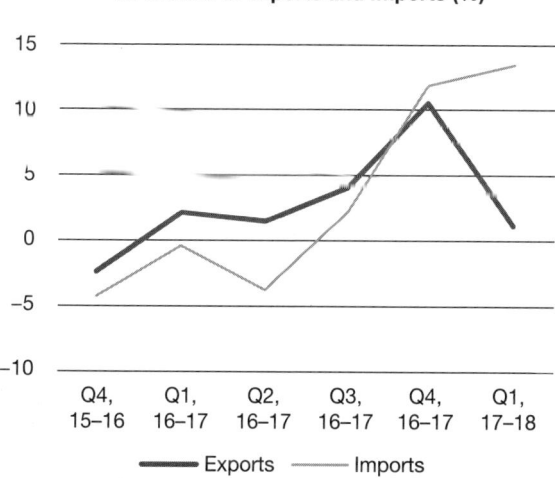

D. Growth of Exports and Imports (%)

— Exports — Imports

D. Export growth has nosedived after the fourth quarter of 2016–17, while the import growth has also slowed down, widening the trade gap, the difference between imports and exports.

Figure 4.2: Contd.

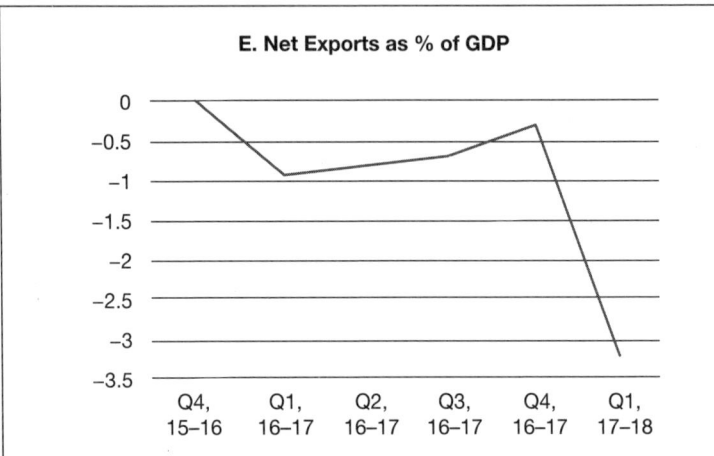

E. Growth of net exports as percentage of GDP has also fell sharply after the fourth quarter of 2016–17 which included the demonetisation period.

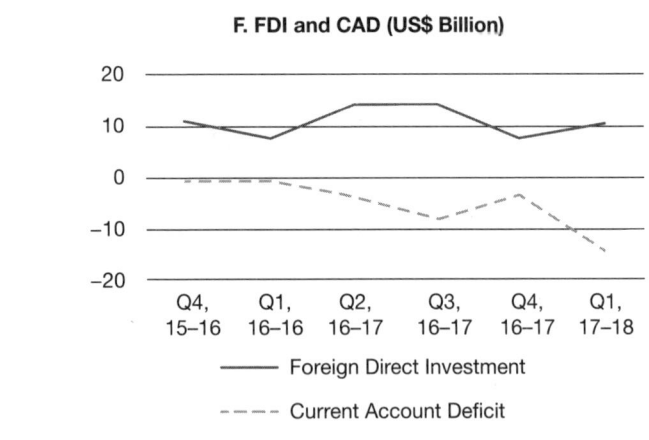

F. While the current account deficit (CAD) took a hit as a result of worsening of the adverse trade balance after the fourth quarter of 2017–18, the FDI improved after that period, reflecting continued faith of foreign investors on the Indian economy.

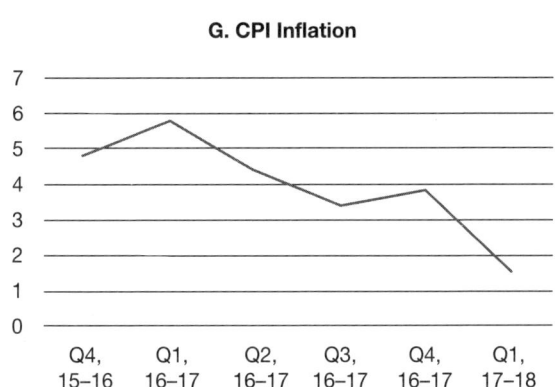

G. CPI Inflation

G. Inflation has been contained well within the monetary policy target of 2–6 per cent and is pretty much under control.

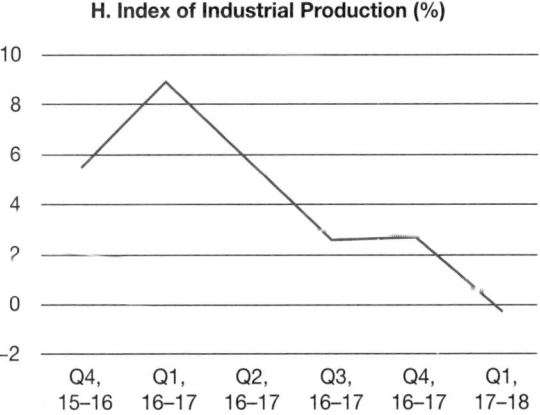

H. Index of Industrial Production (%)

H. However, the Index of Industrial Production (IIP) has been falling almost unabated, except during the fourth quarter of 2016–17, after which it worsened again, perhaps reflecting lower offtake of industrial activities after the demonetisation period.

such as loss of jobs in the informal sector, rural distress and slow growth in employment. But the loss in private consumption after December 2016—due in part to demonetisation— was partly offset by increased government spending which increased steeply after March 2016, and increased from 16.6 per cent in June 2016 quarter to almost double the rate, at 31.9 per cent, in the quarter ended March 2017, before falling to 17.2 per cent in the June 2017 quarter, possibly reflecting the expectation that private investments were about to take off. But even then, the total share of consumption in GDP during Q1, 2017–18, was 66.6 per cent, compared to 64.9 per cent a year ago (Table 4.2). Thus, it cannot be true that there has been any significant fall in the net demand from consumption, either due to demonetisation or GST, to have caused the observed fall in GDP during Q1, 2017–18. There was a decline in the growth of GFCF from 8.3 per cent in Q4, 2015–16, to a negative growth of 2.1 per cent during the quarter ended March 2017, but though growth again picked up to 1.6 per cent in Q1, 2017–18, it is still a long way to go.

Industrial sector (including construction) was, of course, hit the hardest, with industrial growth slowing from 10.3 per cent in the March 2016 quarter to a pathetic 1.6 per cent in the June 2017 quarter. While growth in services had also slowed from 10 per cent in the March 2016 quarter, the fall was not steep at all, and there was, in fact, an increase in the growth of this sector in the June 2017 quarter to 8.7 per cent. Growth in agriculture has picked up after two drought years from 1.54 per cent in the March 2016 quarter rising to almost 7 per cent in the quarter ended December 2016, before tapering off during the next two quarters to end at 1.6 per cent in the June 2017 quarter. But the growth of GVA in the non-farm, non-government core sector points to early signs of recovery, from a low of less than 3.8 per cent in the March 2017 quarter to 5.5 per cent in the June 2017 quarter. This was perhaps due

Table 4.2: Composition of GDP: March 2016–June 2017

	June 2016	September 2016	December 2016	March 2017	June 2017
GFCE	11.3	12.8	10.6	9.4	12.6
PFCE	53.6	53.8	58.6	57.3	54.0
GFCF	31.0	29.4	29.5	28.5	29.8
Change In Stocks	2.5	2.4	2.3	2.4	2.4
Valuables	1.2	1.2	1.2	1.3	3.4
Exports of Goods and Services	20.2	20.4	19.9	21.0	19.4
Less Imports of Goods and Services	22.1	21.2	20.6	21.3	22.6
Discrepancies	-.3	1.2	-1.3	1.6	1.1
GDP	100.0	100.0	100.0	100.0	100.0

Source: National accounts data: Ministry of Statistics and Programme Implementation, 'Quarterly Estimates of GDP at Constant Prices, 2011–12 Series'.

to remonetisation and even though it still remains weak, the worst might just have been left behind. From the previous discussion, it does not appear that the economy is really gasping for breath, as is being made out.

Before GST was introduced, as we have pointed out earlier, fearing the future uncertainty, firms had been clearing off their stocks and consumers had been overstocking. That would have resulted in stoppage of production and slackness in industrial growth along with some rise in consumer demands in the preceding quarters. Immediately after the introduction of GST, the consumer demand, and hence industrial activity, would therefore be low and growth would suffer. Thus, the demand was expected to go down in the quarters following the introduction of GST. Going by this, we may not have seen the worst of growth as yet, and even the second quarter may take a further hit. The economy is likely to do better from the current quarter, October–December 2017, as firms again start restocking after the GST disruption and demand starts picking up again. But since the slowdown had begun well before the note ban, the cyclical downturn may continue for some more time even after the recovery from the twin disruptions caused by demonetisation and GST.

In fact, the October forecast of the RBI confirms this. The RBI has reduced its growth forecast for the fiscal year 2017–18 to 6.7 per cent from its earlier estimate of 7.3 per cent; this is in line with the IMF's growth forecast, which has also cut its growth forecast for the Indian economy by 0.5 per cent to 6.7 per cent for 2017–18. But the RBI thinks that the worst is over. Government sources have cited RBI's estimates to argue that growth would significantly accelerate in the quarters ahead: to 6.4 per cent, 7.1 per cent and 7.7 per cent during the second, third and fourth quarters. The growth during the entire year would be 7.3 per cent as against 7.1 per cent during 2016–17 and 8 per cent during 2014–15. Officially, however, the government has limited itself to saying that it had 'noted' the 'downward revision of growths as well as a slight upward revision of retail inflation'.[10]

Consumer price inflation has fallen steeply from a high of 10.2 per cent in 2011–12 to around 4 per cent now; the RBI expects inflation to move up to 4.2 per cent–4.6 per cent in the second half (October–March) of the financial year and refused to cut the policy rate, though it did not shut the possibility of future rate cuts in view of the expected fall in commodity and food prices which would keep the inflation down. We consider this refusal to cut the rate as an example of unwarranted ultra-conservatism, given the tight leash maintained over inflation during the last several quarters; only about five years ago, 9 per cent inflation used to be the norm.

Its refusal to cut the interest rate substantially is, in fact, partly responsible for the slow growth in bank lending and consequent distress of the small- and medium-scale units. Revival of an economy already distressed by a slowdown would need adequate capital flows into industry which cannot happen without lower interest rates. Inflation has been moving very much within the target policy rate of 4 per cent (+/–2%) for the last several quarters, and it would not have been possible without government's commitment to rein in the fiscal deficit and in maintaining tight fiscal discipline, aided in no small measure by the fall in oil and commodity prices. Optimal economic performance demands both fiscal and monetary policy measures to be applied simultaneously, which, in fact, play supplementary roles.

The inflation scenario, apart from the booming stock market, continues to provide continued assurance about the economy. The retail inflation in September 2017 was 3.28 per cent. It

---

[10] *The Times of India*, 'RBI Lowers GDP Forecast to 6.7% from 7.3%, Says Next Quarters Will Be Better', *The Times of India*, 5 October 2017.

was up from 2.36 per cent in July after reaching its lowest level of 1.54 per cent in June, driven mainly by higher food and fuel prices. In this rise in inflation, again we have seen a replication of the situation witnessed in all countries that had launched GST, and there is no particular reason to feel depressed about the economy on this count. The effective tax on all businesses put together would be lower under the GST regime than before, though their inflationary impact will depend on the extent to which businesses pass on the tax benefits to the consumers. By mapping the GST rates with components in the consumer price index (CPI) basket—which closely represents the household consumption pattern—two economists from CRISIL have calculated their potential impact on inflation. According to them, most mass-consumption goods have been taxed at a lower rate, and several essential food commodities have been exempted. Some items[11] which carry around 20 per cent weightage in the CPI basket could see a one-time transitory inflation hump, while for items that constitute over half of the CPI basket, the tax incidence is expected to remain unchanged. The remaining third of items would see lower tax incidence, allowing for price cuts at the discretion of the manufacturer.[12] The market has actually reflected this scenario, by and large.

In view of the low inflation rate and the likelihood of it remaining more or less unchanged in near future after launching GST, there was a pressing need for cutting the policy rate in order to reassure the economy and also to contain the disturbance caused by it. RBI's stubbornness in maintaining its rate and its fear of an imaginary ghost inflation have, in fact, been

---

[11] For items such as services to higher education institutes, utility bills, personal care products, sugar, prepared meals, snacks and sweets, pan, tobacco and intoxicants, where current inflation is already high, the tax incidence, too, will be higher under GST.

[12] Dharmakirti Joshi and Dipti Deshpande, 'Impact on Inflation: 50% Prices Untouched, 30% Lowered, 20% Increased', *The Times of India*, 26 June 2017.

hurting the economy since the time of Mr Raghuram Rajan, and may have done much more harm to it than good.

However, we agree with RBI's assessment that the onus of reviving the economy lies on the government and more structural reforms need to follow such as closing the infrastructure gap and kick-starting the stalled investment projects, especially in the public sector, recapitalisation of banks for boosting investment and enhancing the ease of doing business, further simplification of GST and addressing the impediments of the housing sector in consultation with the states. The RBI has also warned against any fiscal stimulus to revive the economy, as seen in the aftermath of 2008 global economic meltdown, which could now only lead to unsustainable fiscal deficits.

In fact, the economy is already sending some positive signals. With a near normal monsoon, outlook for agriculture has brightened, and indicators of the services sector are also pointing to growth. Manufacturing, hit by GST, is still causing concern, rendering its short-term prospects a little uncertain but, as already stated, will likely pick up from the third quarter, following global examples of post-GST implementation experiences. As the latest CSO release says, factory output had recorded a sharp rebound in August to touch a nine-month-high growth of 4.3 per cent during the month against a downward revised 0.9 per cent growth recorded in July and −0.2 per cent in June 2017. The surge in industrial production in August was led by the 3.1 per cent expansion in the manufacturing sector, primarily due to restocking of manufactured products prior to the festive season. The mining and electricity sectors also recorded robust performances. The growth in the IIP in August 2017 at 4.3 per cent was a tad higher than the growth of 4 per cent in August 2016 and seems to have bounced back from the negative growth observed in July 2017; however, 13 of the 23 subsectors in the manufacturing sector (with a cumulative weight of 27% in the IIP) witnessed a contraction in August 2017.[13] Exports have started growing since July 2017 and have grown by 26 per cent in September, the fastest in six months, and consequently the trade deficit has also narrowed down to its lowest level in seven months.[14]

In his article 'I Need to Speak Up Now',[15] the BJP veteran and former finance minister, Mr Yashwant Sinha, has used some very uncharitable words to say about the economic reforms including GST. Severely criticising what he calls 'the mess the finance minister has made of the economy', he described the economy being on a downward spiral and poised for a hard landing:

> Private investment has shrunk as never before in two decades, industrial production has all but collapsed, agriculture is in distress, construction industry, a big employer of the work force, is in the doldrums, the rest of the service sector is also in the slow lane, exports have dwindled, sector after sector of the economy is in distress, demonetisation has proved to be an unmitigated economic disaster, a badly conceived and poorly implemented GST has played havoc with businesses and sunk many of them and countless millions have lost their jobs with hardly any new opportunities coming the way of the new entrants to the labour market.

Some of the criticism might have been valid, but as discussed previously, there are already unmistakable signs of economic recovery. If GST was responsible for part of this so-called 'mess', this part is only a transient phase, as international experiences show. In any event, there is as yet no evidence of 'sector after sectors' being in distress. The criticism about GST is rather

---

[13] *The Economic Times*, 'Restocking after GST, Festival Season Push IIP to Nine-month High', *The Economic Times*, 13 October 2017.

[14] 'Exports Grow 26% in September, Fastest in 6 Months', *The Times of India*, 14 October 2017.

[15] Yashwant Sinha, 'I Need to Speak Up Now', *The Indian Express*, 27 September 2017.

unfair, for it is inconceivable that the observed hiccups in such a complex reform were basically a design issue; a perfect design of the GST would have taken an eternity. Logic dictates that it is better to start with an imperfect design and go along correcting it, rather than delaying its implementation indefinitely anticipating problems.

Mr Sinha is also wrong about the prospect of the Indian economy which is resilient enough to withstand and absorb such shocks. Direct tax collections for April–September 2017 have shown a healthy growth of 15.8 per cent over the corresponding period last year. Tax base has widened by 5.4 lakh taxpayers as a direct result of demonetisation, as the second volume of Economic Survey released in August 2017 confirms, bringing additional taxable income of ₹10,600 crore within the tax net.[16] Despite the dismal past trends, exports have registered 25.6 per cent growth in September 2017, far above the 10.3 per cent increase recorded in August. The export sector is always reckoned as an engine to revive economic activity that has remained sluggish due to weak domestic demand, and this is definitely good news. Simultaneously, imports have grown by 18.2 per cent in annual terms in September, below the

---

[16] As per the CAG report of 2016–17, in 2015–16, only 3.98 crore individuals had filed returns. There were 6.9 lakh corporate assesses in addition. To be sure, the number of those who filed returns does not necessarily indicate the number of actual taxpayers, since many of them would be below the threshold. Only 24.69 lakh, or less than 4 per cent of the assessees had reported taxable income more than ₹10 lakh, and paid taxes at highest rate of 30 per cent. Taxes @ 20 per cent were paid by 52.94 lakh, while 2.64 crore paid taxes @ 10 per cent. Of those who filed the returns, 55.93 lakh paid no taxes, their income being less than ₹2 lakh. Of the 76 lakh individual assessees who declared income above ₹5 lakh, 56 lakh were in the salaried class. Only 172,000 people declared income exceeding ₹50 lakh in the entire country. So in a country of population exceeding 130 crore people, only 3.42 crore individuals (2.6% of population) paid any taxes, and only 25 lakh paid tax at the highest rate, about 90 per cent of them from the organised sector where taxes are deducted at source.

21.2 per cent expansion recorded in August, aided by a 5 per cent fall in gold imports. As a result, the balance of trade has narrowed down considerably in September 2017 from US$11.7 billion in August to US$9 billion. Both the external balances—trade balance and current account balance—have improved as a result. Our stock market is on a bull run and the continued healthy growth of FDIs and foreign institutional investments (FIIs) have vindicated the faith of the international community in India's economy, something the IMF Chief Christine Lagarde only recently confirmed while supporting both demonetisation and GST. The slowdown in growth is an expected hiccup, but the long-term efficiency gains will certainly set the economy on a fast course of recovery and lead to higher growth, low inflation, larger volumes of exports and better fiscal health.

Structural reforms are always difficult to implement and are always painful. The pain is necessary to rejuvenate a sagging economy rendered unproductive due to decades of injection of doles and subsidies guided by faulty socialist policies while shying away from big reforms. GST is far from being 'badly conceived and poorly implemented', as Mr Sinha thinks, and it has not affected the India's long term growth potential, as the previous discussion shows.

Mr Sinha was not the only one to have resorted to criticism that was unfair. Another commentator declared,

> By all accounts, two and a half months after it was introduced, GST continues to cause confusion and chaos. Rules are revised with metronomic regularity. Major carmakers have already announced they are cycling back on investment plans in the face of frequent changes in GST rates.[17]

It is too naive to expect that a disruptive and transformational reform, arguably the most complex so far attempted anywhere

---

[17] Chaitanya Kalbag, 'Forget Fast Growth, India is Barely Holding On. Just Look at the Data', *The Economic Times*, 23 September 2017.

in the entire world, will be rolled out with perfect smoothness, without any hitch or glitch and that intended results would be visible within just two and a half months. Are we living in a make-believe world where only the angels tread and things happen as they always should, and where no challenges and crises occur on a daily basis, calling for timely and innovative solutions to respond? Such an assumption would be extremely unrealistic and any criticism based on such assumptions would be too simplistic to merit any serious thought.

Implementation of GST is also throwing up some technological challenges which are affecting the operation of some vital sectors of the economy, especially exports and SME/MSMEs, which demand a closer examination.

Export Sector Challenges

Merchant exporters account for over 30 per cent of India's exports, and they work on razor-thin margins—between 2 per cent and 4 per cent. GST has made their costing calculations go haywire and business operations unviable, especially in respect of products lying at the upper end of the spectrum of GST rates, as they have to pay GST upfront and seek refund after a time lag. In the previous indirect tax regime, they had enjoyed upfront tax exemption on goods to be exported. But now they have to borrow for paying tax while refunds are not available immediately due to glitches in the GSTN architecture as the online facility to claim refunds was still not available until the end of September 2017. Grappling with higher credit cost, and low funds as their working capital had become blocked, many exporters—particularly the small and medium exporters with turnover of less than ₹20 crore—had to postpone their export shipments. The result was a further stress and decline in the export sector already under stress due to slump in demands abroad arising from the economic recession faced by Western countries in Europe and elsewhere, making

Indian exporters even more vulnerable to losing out to their competitors. The apex body of exporters, Federation of Indian Export Organisations (FIEO), is pushing for a complete exemption from import charges on inputs used in the exports.[18] Filing of monthly GST returns is another challenge for small exporters who do not have the wherewithal and technical expertise and have to employ accountants for the purpose, which has raised their business costs further. Other teething troubles also continue to haunt them, one such being related to the payment of the refunds of input tax credit, an issue that had bedevilled all taxpayers ever since GST was introduced.

Although altogether 13 returns are prescribed under GST, there are basically 3 monthly returns (GSTR-1, GSTR-2 and GSTR-3), plus an annual return GSTR-9, that will apply to most resident taxpayers. GSTR-1 includes the details of outward supplies of taxable goods and services made, while GSTR-2 contains the details of inward supplies of taxable goods and services claiming input tax credit. GSTR-3 forms the basis for finalisation of details of outward supplies and inward supplies along with the payment of amount of tax. GSTR-3B—a simple return only for the period from July to December 2017 and not applicable from January 2018 onwards—has been introduced as a temporary measure to make the transition to the new system easy for the taxpayers.

In the initial returns filed in form GSTR-3B, taxes worth ₹92,283 crore were collected for July 2017 from just 64.42 per cent of the total taxpayer base. Of the 59.57 lakh businesses, who should have filed the returns for July, as many as 38.38 lakh taxpayers, or 64.42 per cent of the total businesses who had registered in July, had filed their GST returns. By August-end, the total tax collections had exceeded ₹95,000 crore. Of

---

[18] *The Economic Times*, 'Exporters Seek Quicker Refund, No GST for Merchant Traders', *The Economic Times*, 29 September 2017.

this amount, a staggering ₹65,000 crore pertained to refunds of input tax credit claimed by the taxpayers against the GST paid in July 2017, as well as credit of central taxes paid under the previous indirect tax system. About ₹5,000–10,000 crore of it pertained to exporters.

As per the information booklet prepared by the CBEC on GST for exporters, 90 per cent of the refund amount should be processed within a week of the receipt of the refund application, while the rest 10 per cent would be paid within a maximum period of 60 days. The booklet says that interest at 6 per cent is payable if full refund is not granted within 60 days. Usually, the total GST liability/refund is calculated only when all the three returns—GSTR-1, GSTR-2 and GSTR-3—have been filed. But no exporter got any refund until the end of September, due to technical glitches in the GSTN system. The GSTN system is yet to develop the robustness required to handle such volume of transactions without any glitch, and there is no warning when it will break down due to heavy traffic surges. These glitches have already led the government to push back the deadlines for filing of GST returns repeatedly, from August to October and then to November, delaying tax refunds in turn. The funds of exporters, thus, got locked up unnecessarily, drying up their working capital and hiking up the interest burden.

The delay between return filing and the processing of refunds was particularly harmful to the small companies and the micro and small enterprises as they were forced to borrow additional funds to finance their day-to-day business activities, since they often ended up paying higher interest rates. The effect would make their exports costlier and hence uncompetitive. Engineering goods constitute the biggest chunk in India's overall export basket and are, therefore, vital for job creation, particularly in the SMEs segment. Any stress on these exports would have an immediate adverse effect on the job market, which is already subdued.

As explained earlier, Indian exports were not doing particularly well even during the pre-GST period, with the exports to GDP ratio, an indicator of the relative importance of international trade in a country's economy, down to 20 per cent from its 2013 high of 25.43 per cent at a time when Indian exporters are facing tough competition from countries such as China, Bangladesh and Vietnam in international markets. With the chaos following the implementation of GST, Indian exports might further lose.[19]

Exporters were also facing difficulties owing to ambiguity on benefits available under the new system, which was compounding the problem of refunds further. The Foreign Trade Policy (FTP) 2015–20 has envisaged several incentives based on the earlier levies such as excise duty and service tax, and it was expected that these incentives would be recalibrated under GST. This is yet to happen with no clarity about the incentives, making exporters unsure about the pricing of products set for the EU and the USA. To take advantage of the ensuing Christmas season, it is essential to ensure that goods are shipped in September or at least October to catch that bump.[20] For software export companies, capital goods could include servers, computers and networking devices, among other things. A software exporter from Pune earlier used to save about ₹3 crore in exemptions each year under the government's Software Technology Parks of India scheme, established in 1991 to boost exports. Now, he claims that his company has

---

[19] https://scroll.in/article/851577/no-tax-refund-no-working-capital-how-gst-is-hurting-indian-exporters (accessed on 30 November 2017).

[20] Sachin Dave, 'Exporters Seek Clarity on Incentives under GST', *The Economic Times*, 13 September 2017. However, under the 'Duty Drawback Scheme' of the previous indirect tax regime, the excise duty and customs duty paid on inputs and service tax paid on input services were given back to the exporter of finished products on furnishing proof of export. This scheme was extended for the exporters until September 2017 to provide relief.

already paid ₹25 lakh in import duties in a month, and is still waiting for GST refunds.[21]

The FIEO demanded immediate beginning of the refund process based on GSTR-1 and GSTR-3B data, instead of waiting for all the three monthly returns to be filed completely and data matched by the GSTN system. The government had formed a panel headed by the finance secretary to address and resolve the problem of refunds, which made recommendation to the GST Council.

In the 22nd meeting of the GST Council on 6 October 2017, bringing relief to merchant exporters, the GST Council has fixed a tax rate of 0.1 per cent on goods procured for export purposes and allowed merchant exporters to obtain refund of 0.1 per cent tax paid on export of goods. To prevent cash blockage of exporters due to upfront payment of GST on inputs, the Council approved proposals for providing immediate relief as well as long-term support to exporters. For providing immediate relief, the advance authorisation (AA)/export promotion capital goods (EPCG)/100 per cent export oriented unit (EOU) schemes[22] were extended to sourcing inputs from abroad as well as domestic suppliers, and exempting the holders of AA/EPCG and EOUs from payment of IGST and cess on imports. From 1 April 2018, an attempt would be made to launch an e-wallet facility for exporters to provide liquidity, for which the

---

[21] https://scroll.in/article/851577/no-tax-refund-no-working-capital-how-gst-is-hurting-indian-exporters (accessed on 30 November 2017).

[22] AA is a duty exemption scheme to enable duty-free import of inputs required for export production. EPCG allows duty-free import of capital goods under certain conditions with an export obligation. A 100 per cent EOU is an industrial unit offering for export its entire production. Such units were eligible for various concessions in respect of payment of central excise and customs duties.

Directorate General of Foreign Trade (DGFT) will prepare the norms', to provide long-term relief from liquidity crisis.[23]

As already pointed out, exports have grown 26 per cent to US$28.6 billion during September, showing its fastest pace of expansion in six months. With GST-related glitches out of the way, export performance is expected to improve further in the coming months and reclaim some of its lost territory.

Challenges for the MSME Sector

We have mentioned earlier the fact that threshold for exemption for businesses has been reduced from ₹1.5 crore under the previous indirect tax regime to only ₹20 lakh under the GST regime, bringing many more taxpayers under the tax net, but also offering them the benefit of input tax credit. From Table 4.3, it can be seen that about 99 per cent of the total turnover lies above the exemption threshold of ₹20 lakh, but covers only about 75 per cent of the total entities (60% of corporate entities), individual as well as corporate combined. More than 90 per cent of the revenue will accrue from assessees with turnover exceeding ₹1.5 crore, which also forms the basis for horizontal split between the jurisdictions of the Centre and the states. The reason for low threshold is obviously to cover and track the low-value transactions across the country so as to bring the vast informal sector of the economy into the formal stream, to reduce black money and also to increase revenue from direct taxes. But the large number of micro-entrepreneurs are effectively left unaffected.

It is the SMEs[24]—the primary growth drivers of our economy that contribute almost 50 per cent of the industrial output

---

[23] *India Today*, 'GST Council Gives Relief to Exporters', *India Today*, 6 October 2017. Available at: http://indiatoday.intoday.in/story/gst-council-gives-relief-to-exporters/1/1063326.html (accessed on 30 November 2017).

[24] SMEs are defined as enterprises where the investment in plant and machinery or equipment is between ₹25 lakh and ₹10 crore in case of manufacturing

Table 4.3: Distribution across Turnover

Turnover Range (₹)	Number of Corporate Entities	Percentage of Corporate Entities	Number of Total Entities	Percentage of Total Entities	Total Turnover (₹ Crore)	Percentage of Total Turnover
0–10 lakh	356,036	53.8	6,433,903	68.2	84,964	0.4
10–25 lakh	35,152	5.3	682,859	7.2	111,751	0.5
25–40 lakh	21,875	3.3	325,974	3.5	103,662	0.5
40 lakh–1 crore	51,385	7.8	668,290	7.1	446,671	2.0
1–2 crore	41,455	6.3	503,093	5.3	712,837	3.2
2–5 crore	48,910	7.4	427,039	4.5	1,341,213	6.0
5–10 crore	31,696	4.8	186,931	2.0	1,307,752	5.8
10–100 crore	60,571	9.2	185,503	2.0	4,692,026	20.8
Above 100 crore	14,130	2.1	18,316	0.2	13,726,108	60.9
Total	**661,210**	**100.0**	**9,431,908**	**100.0**	**2,25,26,984**	**100.0**

Source: Press Information Bureau, Ministry of Finance, Government of India, *Report on the Revenue Neutral Rate and Structure of Rates for the Goods and Services Tax (GST)* (4 December 2015). Available at: http://pib.nic.in/newsite/PrintRelease.aspx-?relid=132885 (accessed on 28 November 2017; based on sales turnover data available for 2012–13).

Figure 4.3: Distribution across Turnover (%)

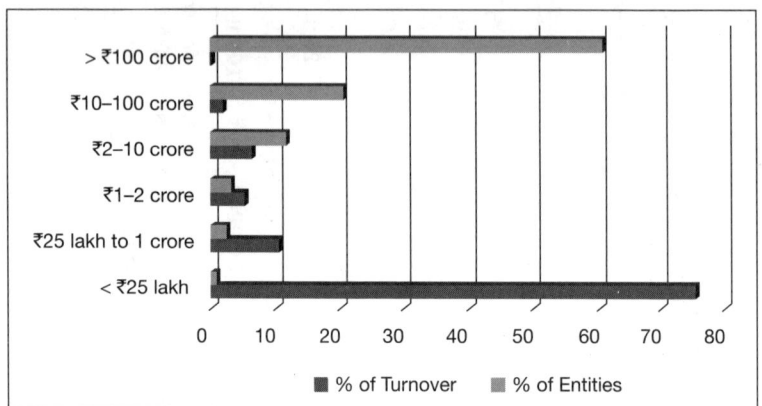

and 42 per cent of our exports—that will feel the pinch of the new tax regime. As per the projections of the Ministry of Micro, Small and Medium Enterprises based on the MSME census conducted in 2006–07, in 2011–12, there were 4.47 crore MSME units, employing 101 million people with gross output exceeding ₹18.3 lakh crore. Almost 80 per cent of the job creation is done by MSMEs, of which 65 per cent is by micro enterprises only (capital investment less than ₹25 lakh). MSMEs create balanced employment across all sectors. GST will now pass on the burden of compliance and associated costs to them while bringing these units under its ambit, but eventually make them more competitive and create a level playing field between large and small entities. That would enable them to compete with foreign competitors from other developing countries such as China, the Philippines and Bangladesh.[25]

---

industries and between ₹10 lakh and ₹5 crore in case of service sector enterprises. Their number is estimated to be around 50 million in India.

[25] Alok Patnia, 'Waking Up to a New GST Era, and Its Impact on Small Businesses in India', 1 July 2017. Available at: https://yourstory.com/2017/07/impact-gst-small-businesses-india-tax-finance-arun-jaitley/ (accessed on 28 November 2017).

GST will, of course, make businesses friendlier to the SMEs, by removing entry barriers, by offsetting the cascading effect of taxes and by market expansion throughout the country. By offering input credit on taxes paid, they will reduce the cost of businesses and increase their competitiveness. However, the major constraints would be the impact of reverse charge mechanism and the increased burden of compliance. Also for inter-state trade, a supplier of goods and services would require registration in every separate jurisdiction, which will multiply the number of returns to be submitted by him, which will add to the compliance cost. Even a 'casual taxable person' who occasionally undertakes supply would require such registration and pay tax at the time of applying for registration on an estimated basis. In case the supplier has no fixed place of business in that state or UT, there would be no output tax in that state, and the SGST cannot be adjusted against input tax credit. To that extent, the tax paid by him would be a sunk cost for such suppliers. For the composition scheme explained earlier, no inter-state supply is again permitted, neither is the benefit of input tax credit available.[26]

But the most damaging to the SMEs would be the reverse charge mechanism we had briefly touched upon earlier. Reverse charge is the liability to pay tax by the recipient of goods or services, or both. Under the CGST Act, a registered unit is first required to pay the tax on behalf of its unregistered vendor or supplier and claim the credit of such tax later. In the earlier regime, service tax laws allowed partial reverse charges where both the service provider and service recipient partially paid the service tax. Under GST, this liability has been cast entirely on the recipient of the service, and this may seriously hurt the small businesses, as large businesses, already reeling under the change management problems triggered by GST,

---

[26] Ibid.

may be unwilling to buy from the unregistered small suppliers and bear the additional burden of paying taxes upfront on their behalf and thereby block their working capital until they can claim the tax credit. Some exemption has been granted by the government for aggregate purchases up to ₹ 5,000 per day from all unregistered vendors, but this limit is too small to be of any help for the small units. They, thus, stand to lose a significant part of their business from supplies made to large units. This defeats the seamless flow of input tax credit through the GST system and threatens the survival of the small units, especially belonging to sectors such as fast-moving consumer goods (FMCG), textile and leather, where a lot of procurement is made from small units including household units. The intention behind the reverse charge mechanism is probably to reduce tax evasion, but it may become counterproductive. The small units may be forced to register with the GSTN, but then their compliance cost will inevitably go up, eating into their small margins.[27]

As explained earlier, most SMEs lack the technical expertise to deal with the online systems of filing of returns and payment of taxes, and would necessarily have to avail the services of tax consultants as well as software-proficient accountants, which would further escalate their cost of doing business. A new feature in the GST regime is the system of 'compliance rating', which assigns ratings to businesses based on their discipline, so that a buyer knows whether his supplier has a 'good or poor' rating before buying from them. This will again hurt the SMEs in particular, as rating becomes 'poor' not just due to a delay in filing data but also due to delays in making payments.[28]

To all these problems are added the lack of clarity about the law and associated complicated rules and procedures,

---

[27] Sudipto Banerjee and Sonia Prasad, 'Small Businesses in the GST Regime', *Economic & Political Weekly*, 52, no. 38 (23 September 23 2017): 18–21.
[28] Patnia, 'Waking Up to a New GST era'.

unfamiliarity with the computerised system and inherent problems of the GSTN, arising from not only its inadequate server
capacity but also security issues which often lead to a system
breakdown or slow response. The CBSE is issuing a series of
FAQs along with other measures to educate the taxpayers, but
it will be a long time before the taxpayers inculcate sufficient
knowledge and confidence about the new system. SMEs, in
fact, had very little time to prepare for GST; they would need
to make heavy investments on technology and its upgrada-
tion. They would become much more dependent now on the
accounting and tax professionals and would have to install ERP
systems to handle the associated technological issues. Most
would find themselves lacking in the necessary resources, and
many may be forced out of business. Thus, for the SMEs, GST
would not be a tale of unmitigated joy, despite its immense
potential of promoting the ease of doing business and reducing cost by eliminating the cascading effect of taxes. It will, of
course, streamline the process of compliance and reduce if not
eliminate the unwelcome intrusion by tax inspectors and consequent harassment at their hands.

In the 22nd meeting of the GST Council on 6 October 2017,
the Centre and the states finally agreed to put in place a new
mechanism to allow those with a turnover of up to ₹1.5 crore—
which make up for about 90 per cent of the total tax base but
only just about 5 per cent of the tax collections but nevertheless are extremely important for job creation—to file quarterly returns instead of every month. The turnover threshold
for businesses to avail of the composition scheme that allows
them to pay 1–5 per cent tax without going through tedious
formalities was also raised to ₹1 crore from current ₹75 lakh.[29]
The finance minister further promised that none of the large

---

[29] At the 23rd meeting of the GST Council at Guwahati on 10 November 2017,
the threshold was further raised to ₹1.5 crore for the composition scheme
with suggestion to amend the law to increase the turnover limit to ₹2 crore.

businesses, which will have to file monthly returns, will be denied credit for the taxes paid by their smaller vendors. Reverse charge mechanism was also deferred until 31 March 2018.

These are important steps to alleviate some of their difficulties, but more needs to be done to make GST a real success and address the problems faced by various players. The online process needs to be simplified with a 24 × 7 helpdesk available to the taxpayers to explain the intricacies in simple language and help them prepare and file their returns in a guided step-by-step process. Until the time the GSTN system stabilises and develops the necessary robustness, or for at least six months or such time considered necessary, refunds may be made by processing the information contained in the returns GSTR-1 and GSTR-3B, and doing away with the necessity for matching the information in GSTR-1 and GSTR-2. Any possible loss of revenue will be a small price to pay for the ease, convenience and assurance it will bring to the small players who may not contribute much in terms of taxes but make a big difference in terms of providing employment; this relaxation may even be made only for them.[30] The implementation of e-way bills should be postponed until the system fully stabilises and starts operating optimally; given the woes of the present computerised system, if every movement of goods requires access to a portal for generation of an e-way bill, it will lead to bigger chaos. Most importantly, the reverse charge mechanism should be duly addressed to make it friendlier to the small unregistered vendors. KPMG

---

[30] The 23rd meeting of the GST Council at Guwahati on 10 November 2017 waived the requirement of filing GSTR-2 and GSTR-3 during the current financial year. While small taxpayers and those with no liability will have to follow a simple two- or three-step filing process, dealers with a turnover below ₹1.5 crore will file only GSTR-1 along with invoices on a quarterly basis. Others will do so on a monthly basis and will follow it up with GSTR-3B for availing the input tax credit.

has suggested a single heading for reverse charge with a single rate, like in the case of classification of machinery imported for a project under a single heading '9801' and levying customs duty on such machinery at a single lower rate. A similar simple solution may be thought of in respect of reverse charge mechanism too.[31]

Where We Stand Now and in the Future

Much has been made of the supposed tax burden on small businesses. However, initial data shows that over about 22 lakh, or 40 per cent, of the 54 lakh businesses which filed GST returns in July had paid no tax at all. Of the remaining 32 lakh businesses, about 30 per cent did not have a cash liability as they opted to use the credits available for service tax or excise that they had paid before GST had kicked in on 1 July. Data further shows that apart from these 'nil' returns, close to 70 per cent of the 32 lakh businesses which had a tax liability paid between ₹1 and ₹33,000 in tax. In contrast, just around 0.3 per cent of taxpayers, covered by some 10,000 companies, accounted for almost two-thirds of around ₹94,000 crore of GST collected by the government in July.[32] Thus, almost 70 per cent of the tax base contributed a mere 2 per cent of the total tax collections. While they may not contribute much to the revenue, they are nevertheless integral to the country's economic ecosystem providing a vital avenue of employment, and it is essential that they are not harmed.

GST collections, however, dipped in August as delayed filing on account of technical glitches took its toll on the overall collection, but recovered somewhat in September (Table 4.4). However,

---

[31] Waman Parkhi, 'GST: Here's What Would Help Its Smooth Implementation', KPMG (INDIA), *Forbes India*, 2 September 2017.
[32] Sidhartha, 'Over 40% Business Entities Make Zero GST Payment', *The Times of India*, 7 October 2017.

Table 4.4: GST Collections during July and August 2017 (₹ Crore)

	July 2017	August 2017	September 2017
CGST	14,894	14,402	14,042
SGST	22,722	21,067	21,172
IGST	47,469	47,377	48,948
Compensation Cess[a]	7,198	7,823	7,988
Total GST	**92,283[b]**	**90,669**	**92,150**

Source: *The Times of India*, 27 September 2017.[33]
Notes: [a]Levied on tobacco products, pan masala and automobiles.
[b]Later revised to ₹94,063 on 26 September 2017 (3.7% higher than August).

the kitty is expected to swell further as more taxpayers are likely to pay late. The compliance rate has fallen in August, with only 37.63 lakh taxpayers out of the 68.20 lakh (55.2% against 64.4% in July) registered for GST filing their GSTR-3B returns. All taxpayers are required to file the monthly GST returns, excluding composition dealers and new registrants for the particular month. The collection is likely to increase as it excludes 10.24 lakh assessees who have opted for the composition scheme. Also, there are still a number of assessees who have not filed their returns either for July or for August, and it may be too early to predict any trend based on these figures due to high claims of transitional credit and pending exporters' refunds.[34] Currently, close to 1 crore businesses and service providers are registered with the GSTN, of which 72 lakh have migrated from excise, VAT and service tax, while 25–26 lakh new taxpayers have been added.

On 8 October 2017, GST had completed 100 days since its launch. While all sectors of the economy have started deriving

[33] Ibid.
[34] *The Times of India*, 'GST Collection Dips 3.6% in August on Delayed Filing', *The Times of India*, 27 September 2017.

benefits from the reduction in the effective tax incidence, streamlining of tax compliance, removal of entry barriers and a seamless flow of credit resulting in overall reduction in procurement and production costs, GST has also brought in additional problems for some sectors. We have already highlighted the problems being faced by the flourishing e-commerce sector. Among the other sectors, restaurants and hotels were found to have largely benefited, and so has the FMCG sector from an overall reduction in the effective rate of tax on most products. For airlines, while the economy-class tickets have become cheaper, the business class travel has become costlier; but airlines are now required to make multiple registrations in different jurisdictions with consequent increases in compliance costs. For the real estate sector, classification of works contracts transactions as supply of service has brought some transparency and relief across the industry, but the rate of tax applicable on most inputs such as paint and cement used by the industry has increased, leading to overall increases in the property prices. This has also been affected by the reverse charge provisions since this sector is typically dependent on a large number of unregistered small vendors like the textile sector which has otherwise benefited due to reduction in tax rate on man-made fibre and yarn. While the reverse charge provisions have been deferred until 31 March 2018, the relief is only temporary. The automobile sector in particular has been a net beneficiary, as GST has subsumed taxes such as automobile cess, infra cess and motor vehicle tax, making for an overall cut in the effective tax rate, though it has suffered from the GST levied on advances, because the tax liability of the supplier arises as advance payment is received, while the credit of such tax is allowed only after goods or services are received, leading to working capital blockage. However, GST on advances for small dealers and manufacturers with turnover up to ₹1.5 crore has now been removed.[35]

Exclusions and multiple rates are always harmful, and the government seems to have acknowledged this at last. Already there is a move to bring the real estate sector under GST, and to reduce the number of slabs. The Centre is now mulling to shift to a single rate of 18 per cent, or a dual slab of 12 per cent and 18 per cent for GST in the future, while states have been urged against seeking too many exemptions and periodic reduction in rates for products and services, as such exemption effectively breaks down the seamless chain for input tax credits; evidence suggests that states still tend to promote their individual interests rather than working towards the goal of a common single market for the entire country. Even when, if, at all, the tax slabs are reduced, it is important to ensure that similar products are placed in the same tax slab; else the scope of unhealthy lobbying will continue to vitiate the implementation, given the unholy politician–businessmen–bureaucratic nexus that is omnipresent in our country.

Even though some tardiness, confusion and glitches have so far hindered the true potential of GST from being realised, it is only a newborn baby, and is still going through its birth pangs. We should allow the newborn baby to grow, mature and gather strength. Fostered by the hopes and expectations of a billion people of a vibrant youthful nation, GST has gathered a momentum within the short period of its existence that is virtually unstoppable and is accelerating its pace towards making the Indian economic system and tax network unified, robust, simple, transparent and accountable. Its promises can be judged from the fact that it has succeeded in crashing even the private moneylenders' usurious rates of interest which have

---

[35] *The Times of India*, 'What 100 Days of GST Meant for Key Sectors', *The Times of India*, 10 October 2017, based on a survey conducted by a team from PricewaterhouseCoopers.

reportedly dropped from 9 per cent to 18 per cent about six–nine months ago to only 6 per cent. Borrowing in the informal market is no more lucrative.[36] It shows the as yet unrealised potential of GST as a game changer, and for driving our informal sector into the formal economic stream.

It is undeniable that GST is the most ambitious and path-breaking economic reform ever undertaken in the country's history. Change is never easy and transition to a new system is always painful. We may derive lessons and hope, from international experiences, to overcome teething troubles as well as to prevent other anticipate problems, to move to a unified single market, controlled by the unhindered operation of a unified architecture. Once the economic benefits from the creation of a common market start flowing, most of the current challenges and glitches will be things of the past we would have happily left behind for good.

Let me conclude by quoting a couplet by Sahir Ludhianvi,

Hazar barq gire laakh andhiyaan utthen,

Vo phuul khil ke rahenge jo khilne vaale hain.

(Even though thunder and lightning may batter it a thousand times, a flower that is destined to blossom will blossom nevertheless.)

---

[36] Saikat Das, 'GST Crashes Even Money Lenders' Usurious Rates', *The Economic Times*, 3 October 2017.

Chapter Five

Goodbye to Tax Terrorism

With the grand ceremonial launch of the much awaited GST at the historic Central Hall of Parliament at midnight of 30 June–1 July 2017, the country entered a new era of tax reforms. It was indeed a giant leap forward towards unification of the fragmented indirect tax structure that was existent so far. Naturally, the expectations were high, emotions all around, and so too were the apprehensions. The road map was ready. The new journey had just begun. In his speech during the launch ceremony, Prime Minister Narendra Modi reiterated that GST will be instrumental in ending tax terrorism. It will help fight black money and corruption.[1] This was a great assurance from the head of the government. Undoubtedly, the implications were enormous.

Since long before the launching of GST on 1 July, a lot of debate had been going on about its efficacy and significance, even though much of such deliberations were marked by partisan and ideological divide. Nonetheless, there were also intense discussions in academic and industry circles regarding the immediate and long-term consequences in the aftermath

---

[1] *The Times of India*, 'GST Is Good & Simple Tax: Modi', *The Times of India*, 1 July 2017.

of GST launch. A policy intervention of such magnitude is truly astounding that independent India has ever witnessed. There is now a continuum of consensus and dissension in political, economic and social paradigm on GST's likely implications. But one thing that everyone agrees is that GST is going to affect each and every individual of the country in a remarkable manner. Even though it is too early to make a comprehensive assessment of its probable trajectory, we can at best try to analyse it from the existing facts and figures. This chapter aims at exploring whether GST will help in ending tax terrorism and in eradicating or controlling the use of black money.

Will GST Actually Eliminate Tax Terrorism?

The government claims that GST will be a strong antidote towards stopping the menace of tax terrorism that is rampant in India. Many people believe that the giant policy reform is going to plug the holes in our fragmented indirect tax system. The nexus between some members of business community and tax officials has traditionally proved to be a powerful force in enhancing tax evasion and tax avoidance, which immensely contribute to tax terrorism. The unification of indirect tax structure facilitated by GST is a bold step forward. GST has definitely emboldened the spirit of 'cooperative federalism', bringing in greater transparency and accountability to the taxpayers, that is, the common people. The purpose is to enhance organised business by creating a level playing field for all. Importantly, GST is expected to significantly curtail the practice/culture of unorganised means of doing business where a big chunk of financial transaction remains unaccounted for. In that context, it is truly a giant step forward in reducing tax evasion, and use of black money, and hence in reducing corruption. Having said that, the pertinent question still to ask is whether GST will be actually effective enough in changing the norms of doing business in the country. The central and state governments have to take adequate steps to enforce GST rules and regulations effectively and to ensure compliance. For that purpose, the primary requirement is dissemination of correct information among common people about the benefits arising out of GST and its compliance requirements. The critical issues to streamline the process of implementation of GST are to ensure reduction and eventual elimination of tax evasion along with elimination of tax terrorism, and of the use of black money as well as administrative corruption.

From a purely societal standpoint, it is important to gauge the effects of GST on our financial well-being. Is it going to impact us favourably or adversely? GST primarily aims at making us all better off. But the onus falls on each one of us—ordinary people; small, medium and large traders; government officials; politicians; and law enforcement authorities—to make sure that the statutory provisions are followed; only then the country can transition to a higher trajectory of economic progress. As of now, there are apprehensions in the minds of people on whether the benefits of GST will actually transpire in their economic well-being, whether it is really going to be a win-win strategy for all and whether tax terrorism be effectively eliminated from the system. These questions are quite natural.

Even if it is too premature to predict anything, still one thing is quite clear—that the majority of people belonging to almost every segment of society is quite upbeat about the prospects of GST, as confirmed by our survey reported in the next chapter. This is something that definitely provides significant impetus and encouragement to the implementation process. Despite the prevalence of positive and negative sentiments, it is clear that most economic indicators that reflect the business trends and market sentiments are hinting towards a better and prosperous living in future. If consumers actually become king and are truly empowered, as GST claims they will be, then that might eventually prove to be the biggest antidote against tax terrorism. But the question is how, when and to what extent can this be done. To answer such questions, there is a need for serious introspection about the immediate and long-term implications of the new tax regime, as GST has already started making inroads into the country's economic system.

A unique feature of GST is that its architecture is designed to ensure compliance through an inbuilt self-policing mechanism. Nevertheless, there is utmost need for addressing the operational bottlenecks and glitches highlighted in the last chapter. GST has the right kind of capability for getting rid of the menace of tax terrorism and black money. Any new policy intervention, particularly of the nature and size of GST, is bound to have initial hiccups and glitches. That is quite natural. However, the hopeful sign is that GST has an inbuilt robustness and adequate safeguards to address such issues in place.

There is a clear purpose in enhancing tax accountability and making the system more transparent. GST aims at eliminating multiple tax components in the production, distribution and consumption channels into a single comprehensive tax umbrella. It enhances the transparency of the tax system as a whole.[2] Under the new system, traders cannot hide any taxable component in the production and distribution network from the tax administration. Simultaneously, consumers will be aware of the basis of their paying the indirect tax at the point of purchase irrespective of the location of transaction. In general, by eliminating the cascading effects of tax incidence through the tax input credit mechanism, GST has already ensured that the consumers will be benefited. In a way, therefore, we see it is a win-win outcome for traders and end-consumers. In this way, the long-term positive effects of the new tax regime are expected to more than offset the possible short-term hurdles

---

[2] K. C. Archana, 'What Is GST Bill? Here's All You Need to Know about India's Biggest Tax Reform'. Available at: http://indiatoday.intoday.in/story/what-is-the-gst-bill-heres-all-you-need-to-know-about-indias-biggest-tax-reform/1/692697.html (accessed on 18 December 2017).

that might arise during the implementation process. GST will also bring more firms into the tax network by reducing the threshold for exemption, thereby increasing the number of goods and services that are to be taxed and hence will enhance the size of effective tax base. That way, the new tax regime is fully capable of weeding out the large-scale tax evasion that was hitherto prevalent in the supply chain. Information obtained in the course of interviews with traders, consumers and tax administrators as discussed in the next chapter confirms that they are by and large hopeful about better prospects under the GST regime.

Side by side, with tax evasion, another bane of the system was tax terrorism. As a matter of fact, tax terrorism has always been a major problem in our indirect tax system. Checks and balances to control it were grossly inadequate. GST is expected to put an end to the inspector raj so ubiquitous in our previous tax administration. GST, in fact, has paved the way for elimination of that inspector raj that has been a bane for our indirect tax system for such a long time. The inspector raj has made the tax system inefficient, non-transparent and non-accountable to honest traders who were paying their taxes regularly. Moreover, it was also a source of corruption and tax evasion, which, in turn, was largely responsible for proliferation of black economy. The problem impacted the whole system adversely in respect of not only sales tax and excise duty inspection but also other taxes like octroi.

Let us explain how inspector raj era became so infamous. In addition to being selective by nature, the inspector raj was essentially based on random and arbitrary checking of traders'/businessmen's books of accounts for tax assessment purpose. There was a complete lack of transparency and accountability during the inspection process in the previous regime in which tax officials could summon traders and businessmen any time to show the books of accounts in support of their tax returns or visit their premises. While doing so, the so-called process of tax assessment quite often became a source of unending harassment for honest traders and businessmen. Because of the prevalence of multiple layers of taxes, the process of such inspection itself was too complicated and extremely time-consuming. In the event of traders' not being able to instantaneously produce proper documentation to tax officials, stringent and unjust obligations were imposed, to escape which one was forced often to bribe these officials. In the whole process, honest traders and businessmen faced humiliation and inconvenience very frequently. The terror and fear of harassment in the hands of tax officials were overwhelming during the previous regime. And tax administration were known for this. But nobody cared for their disrepute. Moreover, there is another angle to the issue of tax terrorism widely prevalent during the earlier tax regime.

Apart from the high-handedness of tax officials, it encouraged building up of a strong nexus between the traders and tax officials that led to the systematic siphoning of huge volumes of unaccounted money from the exchequer. Such nexus in a way acted as catalytic force in the accumulation of black money and proliferation of other financial malpractices. Quite often the big fishes—the unscrupulous traders/businessmen who had connections with tax officials—were left untouched, while petty traders were subjected to untold harassment. Such disturbing trends further aggravated corruption, red tape and nepotism in the tax administration. Detection of such malpractices was extremely difficult because of the complicity of officials, and the vicious cycle of such practices continued unhindered for years. Lack of transparency and accountability characterised the entire system, and the overall consequences of this proved to be enormously detrimental to our economy.

To counter the decade-long maladministration in our tax system, elimination of tax terrorism and inspector raj must now be the top priority of the government. This was even reiterated by Prime Minister Modi during his speech from the Central Hall of Parliament at the launch ceremony, when he said that the new tax regime would usher in a modern tax regime that will put an end to tax terrorism and inspector raj.[3] The assurance of the Prime Minister in this regard is heartening for all stakeholders. When tax terrorism actually gets eliminated, traders and consumers will automatically be empowered. The system would then become more responsive to common peoples' needs and requirements, enhancing their financial well-being at the same time.

That being said, the success of the system lies on its proper enforcement, execution and compliance. The framework of cooperative federalism provides added inbuilt stability to the entire tax administration. It brings the Centre and states together to discharge responsibilities jointly. If both the Centre and states are keen in eliminating tax terrorism, there is no reason why it should not succeed.

The Operational Aspect to Eliminate Tax Terrorism

Under GST, the incentive for traders and business owners is that they can claim input tax credit in the value chain and get benefit of reimbursement for expenses. Automated mechanism is expected to make the system foolproof. The scope of the inspector raj system is replaced by a well-integrated process in the whole production—distribution network. In the new system, the benefits of input tax credit will be carried forward from one trader to another trader down the value chain. This is a big step in eliminating the occurrence of multiple

---

[3] *The Economic Times*, 'One Nation, One Tax Dream Becoming a Reality: PM Narendra Modi', *The Economic Times*, 1 July 2017. Available at: https:// economictimes.indiatimes.com/news/economy/policy/gst-will-chart-new-course-for-nation-pm-narendra-modi/articleshow/59392822.cms (accessed on 13 December 2017).

taxation that was existent under the previous system. However, end-consumers will pay tax as per respective GST slabs. This is how the system is expected to work. To claim input tax credit, each dealer has an incentive to request documentation from the previous dealer in the value chain. Also with the installation of dual monitoring structure as embedded in GST—one by the states and one by the Centre—there will be higher probability to detect incidents of tax evasion. Here, even if one set of tax authorities overlooks and/or fails to detect tax evasion, it will get detected by the other overseeing authority.[4] Thus, there are adequate provisions of checks and balances in place to make sure that tax evasion is detected at any cost in a systemic manner. This will, in turn, help to weed out inspector raj that proved to be arbitrary in nature. Thus, GST has structural competency to effectively handle and eliminate the vices of tax terrorism and inspector raj that were quite problematic under the previous regime.

The backbone of GST is its well-integrated computerised system, commonly known as GSTN, for efficient tax administration. Expectations are that the GSTN is going to simplify the process of tax assessment and appropriation. The online system under GST is already in action in replacing *kaccha* bills (informal/fake bills) by *pucca* bills (formal electronic/ real bills) for any transactions. Automated checks and balances are now being put in place. GST software is doing away with the unnecessary interventions of tax officials. Chances for harassment also now get eliminated with software-driven self-policing mechanism being fully operational. With that, the terror and harassment inflicted by the inspector raj is expected to reduce significantly. Earlier, when there was the prevalence of multi-layered tax structure, there were frequent incidents of

---

[4] Government of India, *Report on the Revenue Neutral Rate and Structure of Rates for the Goods and Services Tax (GST)* (New Delhi: Government of India, 4 December 2015), 4.

dishonest traders issuing kaccha bills to consumers just to avoid paying the legitimate income tax. Such transactions stayed outside account books. Such practices of tax evasion, so rampant earlier, resulted in tax terrorism and generation of black money in huge quantum. On the other hand, there were also honest traders who used to issue pucca bills against all business transactions. Such traders had to maintain proper books of accounts and transaction records for filing their tax returns. They did everything properly, yet many times they suffered from arbitrary harassment from the inspector raj. This was a vicious cycle that is now going to be broken with the introduction of GST. Things are getting transparent and accountable to all stakeholders throughout the entire spectrum of the value chain.

In the earlier system, there was actually no financial integration. Every state had their own rates and own laws. With every state imposing different rates in multi-layered indirect taxation structure, there were multiple taxes and multiple returns filed by traders. Speed and efficiency in transporting products from one state to another were badly affected. With GST, all 29 states and 7 UTs are now working at tandem with each other. Removal of tax loopholes in a systemic manner is the primary objective of GST. With the roll-out of GST, there is one tax throughout the country. Now traders have to register for GST number (GSTIN) to file their tax returns and that too online. Thus, we can see that the entire method of tax assessment and appropriation is now being handled by the GST software. The software will automatically match the data that traders have entered into the system. Traders do not have to separately file return for such transactions. It will be generated by the software itself.[5] Further, when the product moves through the value

---

[5] *The Economic Times*, 'The Biggest Tax Reform', *The Economic Times*, 30 June 2017.

chain and finally reaches end-consumers, they also know how much GST they are paying and on what basis. The electronic system by itself enables a transparent method for tax administration. With the elimination of multiple taxation, the burden of tax on end-consumers is expected to decrease significantly. Consumers now have to pay only their legitimate share. That way the system is just and fair for all stakeholders—traders as well as consumers. The scope for inspector raj perpetuating tax terrorism may become non-existent, if implemented sincerely. The government claims that because of such automatic checks and balances, and self-policing mechanism, the new system is in the interest of common people, traders and industry as a whole. The question is to convince all stakeholders on this matter and bring everyone on the same page for a meaningful public policy convergence.

Is There a Possibility that GST Will Lead to Added Tax Terrorism?

This is an intriguing question that is still lingering in the minds of many sceptics. Even though the government has repeatedly claimed that GST is going to eliminate tax terrorism, there is a need for an objective analysis if there could be a possibility that the new policy instead of eliminating is actually causing more tax terrorism. Under GST, the software-driven tax administration seems poised to substantially reduce the interface between taxpayers and tax officials. That itself is expected to minimise the scope of tax terrorism post GST. However, what if the new system is misused by the same people who are supposed to comply with it in the first place? Will that not lead to revival of tax terrorism in a very different manner even after GST? It might, under the provisions of the anti-profiteering provisions of the GST Act.

There is a possibility that tax benefits under GST enjoyed by traders and dealers may not be passed to end-consumers. For instance, quite a number of consumers are complaining that the benefits of input tax credit are not being passed on to them by traders. As a result, prices still remain high for many products even when there is no hike in their GST rates. Traders are raising the price at the point of sale to consumers in the pretext of GST. This is a gross anomaly that is unnecessarily creating adverse impact on the financial well-being of end-consumers in spite of GST being in place. The implications are exactly the same as tax terrorism, yet now on a different platform—now end-consumers are getting harassed by dishonest traders and ultimately are forced to pay more than their legitimate dues. For example, in just first two days of GST implementation, the Telangana government received over 1,500 complaints of shops, hotels and commercial establishments selling products above maximum retail price (MRP) on the pretext of higher tax slabs. Such businesses were not passing legitimate tax benefits guaranteed by GST to end-consumers. The violation was found to be excessively happening in the hotel industry where there was more confusion due to four categories of GST rates in respect of AC and non-AC categories. Bakeries were also found to be increasing prices of bakery products citing higher GST tax rates.[6] Very recently, in October 2017, a high-level panel of state finance ministers expressed deep concern about frequent complaints of many retailers charging GST on MRP of commodities. The panel recommended the government to make sure that MRP should remain the maximum price of commodities to be sold and if retailers charge anything above this, that would be an offense and attract strict penalty. The panel wanted that GST rule must be applicable to establishments such as restaurants,

---

[6] L. Venkat Ram Reddy, 'GST Misuse: Telangana Govt Receives over 1,500 Complaints in 2 Days', *Deccan Chronicle*, 31 October 2017. Available at: http://www.deccanchronicle.com/business/economy/040717/gst-misuse-telangana-government-receive-over-1500-complaints-in-2-days.html (accessed on 30 November 2017).

eateries and malls that sell packaged products such as bottled beverages which already carry an MRP, but at some places, a GST is charged over and above that MRP. Under all circumstances, MRP should be inclusive of GST.[7] This is a serious problem where implementation of GST is still not able to completely eliminate harassment of consumers. Safety measures need to be geared up accordingly in order to ensure added tax terrorism is not taking place in a different format.

The nexus between traders in the value chain is trying to exploit the ignorance of consumers on GST specifications. This is a major challenge for the government and needs immediate attention. The credibility of the new system will be in question if strict action is not taken by the government to correct the anomaly. Empirical data from consumers reflects that particularly on grocery items, the problem of non-transference of benefits from input tax credit to end-consumers is more prevalent. For example, some grocery items which were sold say at ₹50 earlier are now getting sold at ₹55, despite the fact that there is no hike in GST rates. When benefits of input tax credit are passed on to consumers, the price at which such items are sold should ideally decrease. But on the contrary, it is observed in many instances that just the opposite is happening. Such instances are clear indications that retailers are not passing the benefits of input tax credit to end-consumers. Even tax officials agree that it is a matter that has come to the notice of the government and strict action is required to correct the trend. The gravity of the situation can be ascertained from the fact that the Union finance minister had to warn retailers to pass on the benefits of input tax credits to end-consumers during the 20th

---

[7] *Business Standard*, 'Make GST Inclusion in MRP Must So That Retailers Can't Dupe Consumers: GOM', 31 October 2017. Available at: http://www.business-standard.com/article/economy-policy/make-gst-inclusion-in-mrp-must-so-that-retailers-can-t-dupe-consumers-gom-117103000535_1.html (accessed on 2 November 2017).

GST Council meeting.[8] Hence, we can surmise that tax-related harassment is still going on, much as tax terrorism, but now the victims are end-consumers. At a panel discussion on the occasion of Retailers Association of India (RAI) conference held on 23 August 2017, some prominent retailers agreed about the benefits of passing of input tax credits to consumers; they also reiterated that there was 'lack of clarity on passing on benefits from input tax credit that was unclear at the stock keeping unit (SKU) level'. Unless the government takes strict tangible measures to ensure that benefits of input tax credits are passed on to final consumers, the concept of tax terrorism might still continue in a very different manner.

It was precisely to prevent such a possibility that the anti-profiteering provisions were enacted in the law. It is important to note here that unless the anti-profiteering rules are implemented at the earliest, the possibilities of tax terrorism in the context of traders not passing the benefits of input tax credit to ultimate recipients, that is, end-consumers, will persist in some form, but at the same time it is to be ensured that the coercive provisions are not utilised to harass the honest taxpayers. Clause 171 of the GST Act deals with the anti-profiteering rules. The clause provides that 'it is mandatory to pass on the benefit due to reduction in rate of tax or from input tax credit to the consumer by way of commensurate reduction in prices'.[9] In a way, the anti-profiteering provision mandates businesses to pass on the benefits arising out of lower taxes to the consumer by way of commensurate reduction in prices.[10]

[8] *Hindustan Times*, 5 August 2017. Available at: http://www.hindustantimes.com/business-news/gst-council

[9] ClearTax, 'Anti-Profiteering Rules', 21 July 2017. Available at: https://cleartax.in/s/anti-profiteering-gst-law (accessed on 30 November 2017).

[10] *The Times of India*, 'Next GST Council meet to decide on anti-profiteering mechanism', *The Times of India*, 2 August 2017. Available at: https://timesofindia.indiatimes.com/business/india-business/

In this manner, the clause protects the interest of consumers. In case of failure to pass on the benefits, there will be penalty slapped on defaulting businesses. Since the authority has not yet been formed on initiating the anti-profiteering clause, it is still not operational. Once that actually happens, there will be statutory inspections from time to time to ensure that businesses are actually following the norms and passing the benefits of input tax credit to the final recipients in a legitimate manner. Implementation of the anti-profiteering clause will definitely strengthen the GST nomenclature to safeguard the interests of consumers. But here again there are lots of arguments about the methodology of fixation of reduced prices in the event of reduction of GST rates. Many in the business community are demanding concrete formula to be declared by the government in handling pricing decisions so that penalties may be avoided. Hence, there is confusion there too. Also many businesses have raised reservations against the possible mishandling of the clause once it comes into force. Thus, it is understandable that despite the anti-profiteering clause, there already are many hiccups. Unless proper safety measures are at place, implementation of the anti-profiteering clause may lead to added tax terrorism in the form of harassment of innocent taxpayers. That is a challenge. The government needs to be careful to check such possibilities. For now, since the law is not yet implemented, the possibility of tax harassment down the value chain at the retailer level remains wide open. Thus, critics might still continue to challenge government's proposition that GST is going to eliminate tax terrorism, until an optimal solution to the proper implementation of the anti-profiteering clause is arrived at, with proper safeguards being designed and put in place against its possible misuse.

---

next-gst-council-meet-to-decide-on-anti-profiteering-mechanism/article-show/59875900.cms (accessed on 13 December 2017).

While making a comparison between VAT and GST, it is seen that GST has many safeguards to prevent tax terrorism, but these might not be foolproof. One common argument is that with GST, the cascading effects of multiple taxations will be automatically reduced. That is fine and everybody agrees with that proposition on a subjective level. But let us undertake an objective analysis of the situation. The VAT traders used to file their tax returns every quarter, whereas now under GST, businesses having yearly turnover exceeding ₹1.5 crore have to do it on a monthly basis. So the compliance cost has increased and hence the possibility of unwarranted scrutiny of those returns has not been eliminated especially in the event of mismatch between GSTR-1 and GSTR-2 returns as discussed in the last chapter. Businesses below yearly turnover of ₹20 lakh are exempted from GST. Thus, there are various classifications of businesses based on their yearly turnover with different periodicities for filing returns. Also considering the reality that it takes time to transition for formalisation of business, there is immense possibility of some kind of inefficiency in tax administration even in post-GST scenario. The tendency and mindset of kaccha bill transaction is still there in many traders down the value chain, particularly in MSMEs. Also, when a business of yearly turnover exceeding ₹1.5 crore is trading with another enterprise with yearly turnover less than ₹1 crore who has opted for the compounding scheme, there are challenges bound to happen in reconciling the invoices against sale and purchases. This might further add to the dilemma in the estimation of tax assessment. Filing returns at different intervals of time under GST by different sections of business community is a potent breeding ground for misuse of powers by tax authorities despite the system being handled by software. All such discrepancies under the GST regime need to be addressed by the government with proper safety measures put in place to plug the loopholes that may yet open a new channel for added tax harassment of honest taxpayers.

Will GST Be Able to Curtail Black Money and Corruption?

On the issue of curtailing black money and corruption, the government claims that the self-policing mechanism is robust enough to fight black money and corruption. Safeguard measures such as using the GSTN for raising invoice, claiming input tax credits and filing tax returns will act as catalytic forces in eliminating black money. The government is giving a lot of emphasis on enhancing the efficacy and effectiveness of governance of the GSTN to achieve optimum output. In this context, there has to be a meaningful convergence on enforcement and compliance between government and business community at large. The success of GST greatly depends on the effectiveness of the GSTN because all transactions between various stakeholders, including common people, will be accounted for on this platform. Using software as the backbone of GST is also a serious attempt to gradually transition the informal sector into the formal sector. Black money breeds in a system that is largely unorganised and unaccounted for. Such transactions do not come in the tax assessment network. So the introduction of GST with an automated systemic intervention by itself is a bold and innovative step in the first place on curbing black money. The GSTN is not yet working with full efficiency, as described in the last chapter. The government needs to correct the glitches and put up a foolproof system as soon as possible.

A lot, however, will depend on how GST is implemented at the ground level. Coordination between the central and state governments and other concerned agencies will be critical in assessing the effectiveness of GST in curbing black money. Many traders have a tendency to understate incomes by not reporting each and every business transaction at the time of filing tax returns. That essentially breeds black money in the economy. Since GST will have a paper trail which can be accessed by the income tax department, such practices will discourage generation of black money. Usage of PAN and Aadhaar along with GSTIN will ensure filing of legitimate returns. GST will assist the income tax department to track and detect unlawful transactions. There can be more data mapping for audit by the revenue authorities.[11] Such GST-enabled safeguard mechanism is designed to curtail black money and corruption. That being said, the objective of GST can be significantly strengthened if it is extended to as many goods and services as possible. Currently, alcohol, petroleum products, that is, petrol and diesel, and real estate are excluded from GST. Real estate and alcohol are two biggest sources of states' revenue and black money.[12] Particularly, in real estate, a sector which absorbs and generates maximum amount of black money, the uniform tax structure in the form of GST will improve tax compliance by developers, local builders, property dealers, investors and occupiers.

It is a known fact that black money and corruption go hand in hand. The vicious impact of dishonest transactions is hurting all sectors of the economy. It undermines the right of the common people by eating away their due share. The law-abiding citizens, who pay taxes on their income, as well as the tax authorities equally feel helpless to break the unholy nexus of black money and corruption. Over decades, under a faulty system, there was virtually no mechanism to check unreported income. Various indirect taxes such as excise, sales tax, VAT and service tax were administered by different authorities who had no clue about the extent of unreported transactions. All 29 states and 7 UTs were working as separate entities in indirect tax assessment, with no coordination between them to check the generation of black money.

---

[11] *The Hindustan Times*, 'The GST Impact: How This Tax Will Curb Black Money', *The Hindustan Times*, 4 August 2016.

[12] *The Economic Times*, 'The Midsummer Night's Dream', *The Economic Times*, 29 June 2017.

Introduction of GST will correct such endemic irregularities in the system. It appears to be a foolproof mechanism that will ensure that every transaction is tracked and accounted for from the source until the last stage of consumption. Now it is mandatory to get registered under GST when sellers/traders/dealers cross a threshold limit of ₹20 lakh yearly turnover. Sellers have to upload all transactions based on their raised invoices on to the GST portal. Once the seller uploads details of the organisation's sales to another buyer who is also now registered, the system automatically generates a purchase register for the buyer. System-generated input tax credit is approved for the purchaser. If a vendor fails to upload his sales, it would be at the cost of the purchaser losing the input tax credit. The purchaser will eventually stop buying from a vendor who does not declare his sales.[13] Thus, the new system automatically drives the tax evader out of business as no one will be willing to do business with him. It is in this manner that GST strikes at the source of where black money gets generated. It appears that in-built robust architecture of the GSTN is fully capable of weeding out black money, though the capability is still to be harnessed effectively. The government needs to gear up at all levels to make the system work efficiently through better governance.

The operational mechanism of an automated system ingrained in GST is going to make the tax assessment and appropriation simpler and free of corruption. For instance, if a retailer has purchased goods from a wholesaler, he has to mandatorily upload such a transaction in the GST portal. Thus, to substantiate his purchase, he will have to maintain the books of sales for which proper bills will be generated. A trader will not be able to sell products or goods without electronic (pucca)

---

[13] *The Economic Times*, 'GST: Not Just a Tax Reform, but Real Black Money Law', *The Economic Times*, 16 August 2016.

bills. Once such a bill exists in the system, unaccounted transactions are got rid of automatically. So scope for generation of
black money also gets eliminated. Creating self-policing environment through the GSTN, the taxpayers shall be eligible to
receive input tax credit on a pan-India basis. That would reduce
his net tax liability. Hence, most taxpayers would avoid evasion
in the GST regime.[14]

At the same time, the GSTN is designed to capture all transaction details up to the invoice level. Hence, one cannot escape
the inputs or services used in providing the goods or services.
The paper documentations are to be eliminated completely
in the long term. All the returns of the taxpayers shall be filed
online with the GSTN. They would also get all their refunds,
orders, etc. online. This will decrease the interface between the
taxpayers and tax officials, which would further reduce corruption. The dual monitoring structure proposed within GST,
involving the Centre and the states, will also curb income tax
evasions and corruption at their respective jurisdictions. All
data will be visible to central as well as state government officers. It would be difficult to hide anything or help any corrupt
practices. So even if one set of tax authorities overlooks or fails
to detect evasion, there is the possibility that the other authority will not. Thus, the spirit of cooperative federalism makes
the chances of catching tax evaders more pronounced under
the GST regime. Experts believe that factors such as provision
to declare sales and purchases on the basis of invoices generated, electronic cross-checking of sales and purchases, and
solid IT-enabled GSTN coupled with adequate provisions of
checks and balances are bound to curtail the scope for corruption and generation of black money.

---

[14] GSTinterest.com, 'GST Impact: How GST Will Curb Black Money and
Corruption?' 13 November 2016.

Having said this, the success of GST in the immediate and long-run perspectives will depend on united and coordinated efforts of governments and society at large. Government should be vigilant on the financial irregularities committed by the big fishes in the world of business while showing empathy towards small and medium traders during the transition process. With the roll-out of GST, there might be genuine teething pains for many—particularly small and medium businesses. No doubt, those who were already having a computerised system for maintaining financial and accounting records are facing less hurdles in transitioning to the new system. For the average consumer, the change is pleasing, with lower prices for many products, even though there are complaints of consumers having to pay more for services they do not recall paying earlier for. For instance, some small restaurants that earlier did not mention any tax in their (kaccha) bills are now charging more with the implementation of GST.[15] Such businesses have to generate electronic bills now. Again, the overall tax burden to consumers going to AC restaurants will be higher than those who will be going to smaller roadside food outlets. Notwithstanding such differences, what is important is to bring in larger number of traders into the tax net in order to curb black money. GST is a giant leap forward in that direction. In a country with vast informal sector thriving with a population of 1.3 billion, reforming the system is always painful. Government seems to be aware of this. The exemption announced on a whole host of essential commodities including food staples, milk, flour, fresh unprocessed vegetables, etc. is commendable from social equity standpoint. It appears that there is a consultative mechanism in place to see that people are not left out in the lurch.

---

[15] Lola Nayar, 'Clueless in GST Country: The Teething Period of the New Tax Regime Begins on a Chaotic Note', *Outlook*, 17 July 2017.

Summing Up

The success of GST will greatly depend on how the new tax regime is able to handle tax administration efficiently and make the country free from tax terrorism and black money. According to tax officials, the biggest priority of the government with the roll-out of GST is to make sure that the menace of tax terrorism and black money is reduced to the minimal and eventually completely eliminated. With tax administration becoming more automated because of online recording of transactions and filing of tax returns, the possibilities of interface with tax authorities are minimised. System-generated records will reduce the incidents of raids by tax authorities, retrospective changes of tax laws and reopening of old returns. These are the primary tools that contributed to tax terrorism. Inception of GST also is going to remove unnecessary interference of tax authorities on filing of returns by dealers and creating resentment among those who are not defaulters.

Furthermore, shifting the entire platform of indirect tax assessment and collection to a software-based mechanism provides the tax system with a robust self-policing mechanism to detect any kind of fraud and harassment that might be occurring at the ground level. With all registrations and filing of returns executed online under GST, chances of anomaly in tax assessment are almost negligible. With that, tax officials can no longer be intrusive in financial dealings of traders and also can no longer extort money from innocent taxpayers in the pretext of tax irregularities. Thus, GST has some potent safety measures in place for eliminating tax terrorism. Its self-automated policing system should eliminate the possibilities of arbitrary selection of traders for the purpose of verification of their books of accounts, which often were sources of harassment of honest taxpayers in the first place. With the launch of GST, no tax official is now authorised to visit the premises of traders and shopkeepers without the prior permission of competent authority in a bid to reduce unnecessary harassment of taxpayers. All these are major steps forward in reducing the menace of unpopular inspector raj that was so widely prevalent earlier.

On the issue of reducing black money also, a fully automated system with robust self-policing mechanism brought in by GST has enhanced transparency and accountability of tax administration. With the online reporting of every transaction and inbuilt computerised invoice matching system, the tendency/scope of people to sell without invoice is likely to be reduced significantly. Under the new tax regime, every supplier has to upload an invoice in order to reap the benefits of input tax credit. In case the supplier does not want to sell with a software-generated invoice, no registered buyer will be buying such seller's products. In this way, GST has plugged the holes in the system in such a manner that there is lesser scope for unaccounted cash transactions, which is the root cause of generating black money. It is in this way that GST is expected to eliminate the generation of black money. With GST thus establishing a tight hold over black money, the level of corruption is also likely to be brought down and ultimately eliminated. Another factor that would reduce black money is the reverse charge mechanism where there is some kind of systemic pressure for bringing unregistered traders under tax network, as discussed already in the last chapter. All these measures under GST have the power and capability to curtail black money and corruption significantly.

Finally, we all will agree that the success of GST is ensured if people from all walks of life—traders, business community and end-consumers—feel themselves comfortable with the new system and are convinced that it is going to increase their financial well-being. For traders who were earlier maintaining only ad hoc records and were mostly transacting in cash without paying taxes, the new system under GST seems too intrusive for such evasion as it maintains records of each and every transaction, and this might initially cause some discomfort and resentment in the minds of traders and dealers, but there are also some genuine difficulties. The last three and half months since the roll-out have seen incidents of protests in an increasing number of cities, starting from Surat, Varanasi, Bhopal and Coimbatore, among others, mostly by textile traders. These are traders who work with very little capital, take goods on credit and take credit risks. Many of them did not have any installation of computerised system in their business. GST has hit them rather badly. Most of them did not maintain books, so there was no transparent reporting. Only once a year would they sit with their chartered accountants and sort out their finances and file returns, if at all. Definitely there is a need to get them into the tax net, but at the same time without forcing them to close business. Adequate awareness and computer training facilities should also be extended to them by government, semi-government and non-government organisations for hassle-free transition to formal system of business. Once all categories of people realise that GST is going to usher in an era devoid of tax harassment, the system itself will become a success. The fundamentals of GST are very robust. With its proper implementation, execution and compliance, it is bound to make everybody's life better.

Chapter Six

Voice of the People

Ever since its launch, GST has been the central focus of the ongoing socio-economic discourse. The moot question is how it will impact everyday life for the stakeholders. While traders and businesses have been wondering about their tax liabilities and profitability, the common people have been thinking about their daily budget and changes that they need to make in their spending plans. Government has been monitoring and assessing its overall impact on the economy. The contest between long-term economic benefits and short-term hardship is distinctly visible. This chapter attempts to analyse the implications of GST based on our interactions with the various stakeholders in order to assess if the apprehensions in their minds are true in the light of emerging reality, and how GST is going to impact common people's economic well-being and the traders' business prospects. In the process, the chapter also endeavours to examine the claim that GST will actually result in creating one market throughout India.

It is by now appreciated by all stakeholders that GST is a landmark structural economic reform that impacts all of us in one way or the other, though the nature of such impact varies for different stakeholders across the board. There are several reasons for such diverse responses. Regional economic imbalance, cultural traits, customs and practices, food habits, social configuration and associated public space domain, etc. play their parts in the diversity of responses obtained from the stakeholders. With the implementation of GST, there are variations in tax rates depending on the classification of goods and services; some are charged GST at higher rates than others. Also, for many products there are no changes in tax rates, while some essential commodities such as milk, food staples, unprocessed vegetables and flour are exempted from GST. However, some services sectors are going to experience higher tax rate of 18 per cent as compared to the earlier rate of 15 per cent, but with lesser complications and enhanced transparency and accountability in the new system. For instance, in the earlier fragmented regime of indirect tax system, service sector was adversely affected with multiple taxes comprising VAT, service tax, Swachh Bharat Cess, Krishi Kalyan Cess and service charge. Variations were multidimensional in different categories. Cascading effects of multiple taxes used to blur transparency of the tax system. It also led to unnecessary hike in the overall tax that consumers had to pay as end-users, most of the time without any clarity. In contrast, under the present GST regime in both goods and service sectors, all multi-layered indirect taxes are now replaced by one GST rate, which is clearly visible in the invoice, split between CGST and SGST for.sales within states.

GST is, thus, a remarkable policy intervention that affects all stakeholders in different ways. No analysis of this massive policy reform could be complete unless it is backed by some empirical evidence. Realising this, it was decided to conduct market survey to assess the reality from the real-life experiences of the people which is the ultimate test. The survey was designed to be exploratory in nature, keeping in mind that this reform has an all-encompassing scope and magnitude.

Methodology of Survey

To get a holistic picture of the market, field investigation and interviews were carried out among traders, business owners, consumers and tax administrators. The market survey was conducted based on purposive sampling for qualitative evaluation. The approach was adopted to assess the dynamics of all those sectors that are traditionally characterised by high consumer interface and footfall.

Although it was a very limited survey, given the limited resources in terms of time and manpower available with us, we had attempted to make it as comprehensive as possible in terms of coverage by collecting real-time information and opinions from a representative sample. For that purpose, 53 different stakeholders from diverse segments were interviewed/interacted with in Delhi/NCR area between 22 September and 31 October 2017. Timeline was specifically selected keeping in mind to cover the busy festive season of Dussehra and Diwali when sales are at the maximum. With some 20 stakeholders comprising traders/businesses/shop owners/managers covering diverse businesses and sectors and 33 consumers belonging to different segments of society, the field investigation attempted to obtain a holistic picture of the present state of conditions in the market after the inception of GST. A preliminary questionnaire was used for the survey, followed by detailed personal interaction with each respondent. None of the respondents were known to the interviewers personally, and most of the respondents preferred to remain anonymous. The evaluation is qualitative; any quantitative analysis was not within the scope of our survey.

Table 6.1 summarises the various categories of traders/ businesses who were interviewed during the survey.

Table 6.1: Sample Details: Traders and Businesses

Category	Sector	Number of Respondents
Proprietor—Business	Salon Chain	1
Business—Managerial	Restaurants, Cafes and Fast Food Centres	5
Trader—Manufacturer	Hosiery and Textile	2
Trader—Shop Owner	Gift Items	1
Trader—Shop Owner	Grocery (Kirana) Store	1
Shop Owner—Managerial	Pharmacy Store	2
Trader—Shop Owner	Optical Store	1
Managerial	Automobile Services	1
Managerial—Transportation	Courier Services	1
Trader—Shop Owner	Electronic Products	1
Trader—Shop Owner	Electrical Products	2
Proprietor—Business	Home Appliances	1
Managerial	Mobile Phones	1

Table 6.2: Sample Details: Consumers

Category	Number of Respondents
Working Ladies–Housewives	9
Working Men	8
Undergraduate Students–Young Generation	6
Postgraduate Consumers	3
Lady Teachers	2
Young/Middle-aged Working Executives	2
Retired Senior Executive in Private Sector	1
Accounting Professional	1
Retired Army Personnel Currently Working in Private Sector	1

Table 6.2 provides a composite picture of the various categories of consumers who were interviewed.

The survey was conducted in small- and medium-sized marketplaces, shopping malls, office complexes, busy restaurants and cafes, university campus, households, manufacturing units, service centres and small shops/business establishments to make an inclusive coverage of the representative sample.

Even within the constraints of limited time and small number of respondents, we were able to get some interesting insights and identify trends that reflected the dynamics of market. The observations/findings from the survey in a way echo the voice of the people at large, belonging to all walks of life.

General Perception among Stakeholders

Looking at a cross section of people from various walks of life through actual field investigation, it was seen that GST brings in with it a mixed bag of reactions and counter-reactions. While some segments of population seem optimistic about the future prospects of GST, others are cautious and not much excited. Some are quite critical about GST as well. This has been the general trend found in the responses. However, in general, the mood of the people was seen to be more inclined in favour of GST rather than against it; even those opposing it admitted the potential benefits of GST when, and if, it stabilises. Majority of the respondents are perceived to trust the government's assurance that GST will bring in significant economic benefit in the long run; they are willing to give more time to the new indirect tax regime to unfold its full potential. Although it is an oscillation between hope and apprehension between different stakeholders—be it the government, common people or business community—nevertheless, overall impression we gathered is that there is certainly a strong, yet cautious, undercurrent of optimism about the future benefits of GST.

In contrast to all other previous tax systems, the backbone of the GST regime is its software-regulated tax administration capabilities. Under the new system, all transactions are to be accounted electronically. There are also some technological glitches that are surfacing from time to time in the operation of the software. Our field investigation shows that despite hardship being caused by the GST software-related problems coupled with somewhat tedious experiences at the time of filing returns online, the traders and business community are cautiously upbeat, barring some exceptions, about future benefits of GST. At the same time, consumers are trying to assess the impact of GST on their daily lives. However, by and large, the consumers are also positive on the future prospects of GST. There are also those who are highly sceptical about GST as it has impacted their budget and economics adversely and for good reason. These are challenges before the government on the execution of the new policy, which are causing genuine difficulties and disappointments among such stakeholders. A few of the respondents are also undecided at this point of time, as it is too early to come to any conclusion about the positive or negative impact of GST. The government is presently trying to be responsive to the needs and requirements of the market and is trying to make necessary adjustments in the tax administration. We understand that these are early days to come to any finality or judgement; the responses can at best describe the interim transitional scenario. Nonetheless, our overall assessment from qualitative evaluation is that even though there are serious and genuine concerns and problems affecting most stakeholders, there is still a sense of positivity in the market about the future benefits GST will bring. None advocated a rollback, and some of the stakeholders, particularly consumers, expressed the opinion that GST should have been implemented much earlier.

Voice of Business Community Post GST

During the course of multi-sectoral market survey, diverse groups of traders/business owners were interviewed to assess the market dynamics post GST. The narratives are insightful and revealing; they, by and large, reflect the market sentiments with regard to trades and businesses, giving us some idea about the actual state of conditions since the inception of GST. We present the sector-wise summary of the narratives of business community in the succeeding sections.

Restaurant Business (Lunch–Buffet–Dinner Chain)

With regard to restaurant business, we visited a premier restaurant chain in Delhi/NCR as part of our field investigation to assess the current status post GST. According to the manager at the business premises, GST has not resulted in any significant change in business volume so far. But the tax structure in the restaurant business under the GST regime has not only become simpler, but the tax burden has also become less as compared to the previous VAT regime. For instance, prior to GST, restaurant businesses were subjected to VAT at 13.5 per cent, service tax at 5.5 per cent, Swachh Bharat Cess at 0.2 per cent, Krishi Kalyan Cess at 0.2 per cent and service charge at 10 per cent. Hence, in the pre-GST situation, the total amount of indirect tax to be paid by customers came to around 30 per cent. However, in the current GST set-up, there is only 18 per cent tax equally divided between CGST and SGST at 9 per cent each. Hence, in the present situation, end-consumers end up paying less amount as tax for dining out in a restaurant. The restaurant business is upbeat that in the long term, GST will be enhancing the net profitability, at least in the organised sector business domain. At the same time, customers are also getting to know how much they are paying as legitimate tax which is clearly mentioned in the invoice. This is a win-win outcome for both restaurants and consumers.

While organised sector restaurant business is transitioning to the GST regime in a relatively satisfactory manner, the scenario is very different in the unorganised segment of the restaurant business. Field conversations enabled us to realise that the problem of kaccha bills is still widely prevalent in majority of cases. Many of the unorganised restaurants such as roadside dhabas or even open food stalls with sign boards are not paying tax to the government as per the GST rules. On the contrary, they are collecting GST from the customers and still issuing kaccha bills. Such businesses are still not registered with the GSTN, yet they are charging GST and inflating prices. They are taking advantage of consumers' ignorance and lack of awareness. Cash transaction is rampant in the informal sector. A tax administrator interviewed by us also agrees that things are not happening as per rules in the informal sector and that the government needs to take action to correct it.

It is necessary and important to bring such traders under the ambit of GST. Otherwise, the credibility of the GST regime will be affected. Thus, there is large grey area that needs to be handled promptly and efficiently by the government in respect of this sector in particular.[1]

Sweets, Namkeens and Restaurant Services Other than Lunch–Buffet–Dinner Chains

Let us now analyse the scenario in respect of the sweets and namkeen shops as well as ordinary restaurants other than the lunch–buffet–dinner restaurants discussed earlier. Our field investigation shows that a leading chain in this category is cautiously optimistic about the future business prospects post GST, while reactions are mixed on its implication from others. Earlier, sweets and namkeens were taxed at 5 per cent each. Now after the roll-out of GST, sweets are still taxed at 5 per cent (CGST at 2.5% and SGST at 2.5%). However, now namkeens are taxed at 12 per cent (CGST at 9% and SGST at 9%). Therefore,

---

[1] The 23rd GST Council meeting at Guwahati on 10 November 2017 has reduced GST on restaurants to only 5 per cent but without the benefit of input credits.

while in the sweets segment the situation remains unchanged, namkeens have become more expensive in the GST regime. It is also important to notice that these rates are just for the take-away items; if the customer wants to sit in the restaurant and consume the same products—sweets and namkeens—then a much higher GST rate at 18 per cent will apply (CGST at 9% and SGST at 9%). Such discriminations have been introduced post GST, which look like an aberration.[2]

But despite such variations in rates, shops and restaurants agree that GST has made the system simpler and more transparent. In the previous set-up, some products were not identified and proper tax rates were not fixed for them. Under the GST regime, most products have HSN Codes that specify appropriate GST rates.[3] So it is difficult to evade tax now. The manager of a chain has confirmed that GST has actually simplified tax calculation. For the customers also, it has brought clarity about the tax components. Earlier, a customer had to pay VAT at 13.5 per cent and service tax at 5.5 per cent. In total, the tax charged from the customers was @ 19 per cent, excluding various other cesses and service charges. Now GST tax at 18 per cent has benefited the customers as they virtually pay less. At the same time, the pucca bill nowadays issued clearly mentions the GST rates for various items/services used along with HSN/SAC[4] Codes for individual items purchased. This has

---

[2] However, milk products such as *chhach*, curd products and paneer (cottage cheese prepared from milk) attract no GST. Baked paneer and branded paneer attract a 5 per cent GST.

[3] https://www.taxmann.com/blogpost/2000000082/what-is-hsn-code-under-gst.aspx (accessed on 30 November 2017). This type of classification is used for taxation purposes in identifying the rate of tax applicable to a product in a country. This code is also used to determine the quantity of item traded or imported all through a nation.

[4] The SAC means Services Accounting Code under which services that fall under GST are classified. HSN Code and SAC are the codes used to classify goods and services under the GST regime in India.

certainly enhanced transparency, benefiting both businesses and end-customers. The company official has expressed his satisfaction with such developments but also pointed to the problems encountered with the GST software. Many a time, the GST website is found to be down and that has created serious hiccups in entering data on transactions and in filing of returns. If the technological anomalies are removed swiftly, only then GST will be a big leap in the right direction in the area of B2C operations, the official added.

As regards the B2B transactions, under GST, any transfer of products from one company location to another company location in a different state has to be accounted for via IGST which attracts a levy of 18 per cent. Here, each of these company locations will be treated as separate offices, unlike in the VAT regime. For example, if a company office in Delhi is sending food consignments of an amount of ₹1,000 to another company office in Gurugram, then IGST at 18 per cent will be levied. The Gurugram office will pay ₹1,180 to the Delhi office. The Gurugram company outlet will charge GST from the end-consumers at 5 per cent, 12 per cent and 18 per cent, depending upon the item/service traded. Thus, we can see that while the Gurugram office outlet is paying the Delhi office at 18 per cent IGST, they are collecting GST from end-consumers at 5 per cent, 12 per cent and 18 per cent, as the case may be. The reconciliation of accounts between the Delhi office and the Gurugram office should be automatically done through the GSTN software, and the remaining tax obligations post reconciliation, if any, will have to be paid by the company head office to the government. That is how GST is supposed to be implemented for restaurant chains in the business of sweets and namkeens having outlets in different jurisdictions across the states. This reconciliation remains quite problematic as of now.

The company official also deliberated that until the stock of items having previously quoted MRP is fully sold out, profits and losses will remain a little uncertain for the business. In the medium and long terms, when the new/revised MRP will be revised by making adjustments for the GST rates, the input tax credit will balance out for consignments moving across states. That will further formalise tax administration. Under the previous VAT regime, many items were not identified and tax rates were not fixed for them. Cascading effects of multiple taxes were detrimental to businesses, and there was lack of transparency for both businesses and customers. Also at the time of shipment of products from one branch to another branch office, tax calculations were done on the basis of inter-office transfers. There was lack of clarity on the taxable value of the shipments and net tax proceeds, often leading to tax terrorism by inspectors. All these drawbacks have now been things of the past under GST. The only red flag is the GST software glitches which the government needs to correct at the earliest.

Fast Foods and Coffee Chains

While interacting with an extremely popular fast food and coffee chain operating on a pan-India basis, we were told that there is no significant impact on their business volumes so far post GST. Items such as coffee, tea, burgers, sandwiches and samosas are all currently traded virtually at the same price. The company has not made any changes in MRP for such products so far. On the contrary, for some packed items such as guava juice and banana chips, the company has fixed its MRP one rupee cheaper.

When we visited another coffee chain that is an internationally acclaimed brand name by itself, we found that the bill generated is very systematic with detailed information on HSN Code for the services delivered, CGST at 9 per cent, SGST at 9 per cent, taxable value on items purchased by end-consumers and the tax amount as well as the net payable amount.

For example, HSN Code for majority of goods and services provided by restaurants, cafes and similar eating facilities including takeaway services is 996331.[5] Based on the identification of the HSN[6] Code, GST rates are automatically fixed. There is no separate mention of service charge that used to confuse the consumers during the VAT days. The bill also mentions GSTIN of the store. Another outlet of a different coffee and fast food chain operating on a pan-India basis also showed the same systematic billing procedure with HSN–SAC[7] clearly stated along with GST calculations and rates. Similar to the chain mentioned earlier, services related to food and beverages served in restaurants, cafes and similar eating outlets (commonly known as fast food centres) showed the HSN–SAC as 996331. Trends obtained so far by visiting the restaurants and cafe chains revealed uniformity in the pattern of billing process with tax overheads clearly stated along with the HSN and SAC Codes, reflecting the enhanced transparency regarding tax components that GST has brought for the consumers.

Salon Business

With regard to the salon business, representatives of a premier salon chain have indicated that the launch of GST has not

---

[5] https://www.gstbazaar.com/sac-codes/code/996331 (accessed on 30 November 2017).

[6] https://www.taxmann.com/blogpost/2000000082/what-is-hsn-code-under-gst.aspx (accessed on 30 November 2017). This type of classification is used for taxation purposes in identifying the rate of tax applicable to a product in a country. This code is also used to determine the quantity of item traded or imported all through a nation.

[7] SACs are used for GST classification. This service comes under food, edible preparations, alcoholic and non-alcoholic beverages serving services, distributive trade services, accommodation, food and beverage service, transport services, gas and electricity distribution services. Heading number of such service is 9963 and the group number is 99633. These codes are mandatory for mapping or classification of services that need to be used by a taxpayer.

really affected their business. On the contrary, they are happy that now the indirect tax structure is made more transparent both for them and for their customers. The monthly volume of business has remained the same in the post-GST era. There has been no change in the tax rate of 18 per cent in salon business before or after GST in Delhi. However, in places such as Gurugram which fall in Delhi/NCR, while the indirect tax component was 15 per cent earlier, under GST it has been raised to 18 per cent. Hence, if the price for normal haircut and colour earlier was say ₹1,500 in Gurugram, then with the tax it became ₹1,725. Today with GST at 18 per cent, the total cost to end-consumers for the same service is ₹1,770. This is a nominal increase for their customers, and the salon chain has not witnessed any tangible change in the business volume so far post GST. The representative in the salon chain says that under GST, the billing process is simple and transparent for both business and consumers. The representatives of the salon chain are upbeat that in future, their business is expected to earn higher revenue and profitability across the country because of the uniform tax structure under GST.

Hosiery, Textile and Gift Shop

During the course of field investigation in organised garment shops and multidimensional gift item stores, we found that many small- and medium-sized traders have made a transition into the GST regime. This has definitely increased the number of tax assessees in the indirect tax network. This is no doubt good news for the government. At the same time, such traders are generally satisfied with the efficacy of GST. The shop owners said that in the earlier system, there used to be tax evasion at the time of buying inputs due to rampant kaccha bill trading. With the roll-out of GST, things are much more formalised and systematic. Sellers and buyers have to maintain proper records of transactions and match their invoices in accordance with respective

GSTINs, since only by doing so, the benefits of input tax credit can be claimed. Also, in the current system, there is proper transparency for end-consumers on the GST rates and the amount of tax that they are supposed to pay. While some products have become more expensive, some others have become cheaper depending on the GST rates fixed by the government. But the overall impression reflected by shop owners can be considered favourable for GST. However, one concern among traders in the organised sector is to manage the reconciliation of the discrepancies between the MRP of old stock (which were still existent when fieldwork was undertaken) and the current GST rates in such a manner that end-consumers are not unhappy. As a result, traders are not able to transfer the benefits of new GST rates on end-consumers all the time. Traders think that such disparity may create some temporary problems for the consumers or loss in revenue, but they are optimistic that once the old stock is sold out and new MRP comes into effect, things will normalise. The new MRP will be fixed keeping in mind the GST rates for various products to even out any loss factor. As per Table 6.1, we found an underlying current of cautious optimism on GST. Traders resonate confidence in the GST regime. Interestingly, some of them do not even complain about the technological glitches in GST software. Such traders are of the opinion that they are now having a level playing field in terms of doing business since all transactions are in black and white.

Apparel and Textile Manufacturing Unit

With regard to apparel and textile manufacturers in the post-GST era, our investigation suggests that things remain more or less unchanged. When questioned, a representative of a textile manufacturer confirmed that they have transitioned to GST system quite comfortably. Their business prospects are also currently satisfactory. GST tax rate for textile products is 5 per cent (CGST and SGST at 2.5% each). The company representative emphasised that they do only job work in tailoring the apparel based on the contract received from domestic and international clients. Once the textile manufacturing company gets contract from domestic clients for tailoring activities, they complete the job work within a stipulated period of time. They then hand over the final product to clients by charging 5 per cent GST. For example, if the contract price is ₹1,000, then the finished textile product is to be delivered to the client with a total price of ₹1,000 plus 5 per cent on ₹1,000. The total amount due from the client is ₹1,050. Once the invoice is uploaded by the textile manufacturer and the payment is subsequently received from the client, the consignment is delivered. For shipment to international clients, the apparel manufacturer raises the invoice and sends the material to the clearing house. They claim the input tax credit and get reimbursement from the system. The clearing house makes arrangement for consignment exports and the payment of sales proceeds to the manufacturer. The same is true for other apparel and textile manufacturers. According to industry veterans, an extension of modest GST to both fabrics and apparel will lead to a very substantial expansion of the tax base—just a 5 per cent GST can expand revenues almost threefold according to some. Voluntary compliance of GST provisions in apparel export business is also likely to grow.[8] Thus, there is optimism in the apparel and textile industries post GST despite some traders in Surat, Varanasi and Mumbai resorting to protests earlier. The protests seem to have been caused by the fact that the new system hurts their traditional kaccha trading practice which facilitated tax evasion.

That being said, there are some technical glitches in the apparel export sector. According to a company representative

---

[8] ETRetail.com, 'Textile & Apparel Industry Looks Keenly at GST Rates', 1 June 2017. Available at: https://retail.economictimes.indiatimes.com/news/apparel-fashion/apparel/textile-and-apparel-industry-looks-keenly-at-gst-rates-on-june-3rd/58941383 (accessed on 7 November 2017).

interviewed by us, the documentation work is quite tedious. The government should take steps to further simplify the documentation and reimbursement of input tax credit for promoting exports of textile products.

Garment Departmental Store

When a large-size garment departmental store was visited during the course of market survey for taking a look at the general business practices adopted post GST, it was observed that GST rates were implemented based on HSN Code and invoices raised accordingly, showing the HSN Code for items sold, CGST and SGST at 2.5 per cent and 6 per cent for different items each, the MRP, tax amount and the net payable amount.

It was observed that in the garment sector retail chain, there have been different products with different HSN Codes and different GST rates. For apparels and clothing accessories, knitted or crocheted, of sale value not exceeding ₹1,000 per piece, the GST rate is fixed at 5 per cent, whereas for similar items of sale value exceeding ₹1,000 per piece, the GST rate is 12 per cent. HSN Code for such items is 61. Again, GST rates for apparels and clothing accessories, not knitted or crocheted, of sale value not exceeding ₹1,000 per piece is 5 per cent, while for articles of apparel and clothing accessories, not knitted or crocheted, of sale value exceeding ₹1,000 per piece GST rate is 12 per cent. HSN Code for such items is 62. The practical implementation of this was verified from the invoice generated. We gathered an impression of systematic trading going on in a large reputed garment departmental chain with no confusion or hidden charges and that complete transparency was maintained.

Grocery (Kirana) Store

While visiting a grocery shop, we saw that there are not much changes in the tax rates in respect of majority of grocery items.

In the previous system, VAT and associated cesses together attracted taxes at the rates of 5.25 per cent, 13.25 per cent and 18 per cent in respect of different items. In the current GST regime, the tax slabs have been fixed at 5 per cent, 12 per cent, 18 per cent and 28 per cent.[9] There are some changes in the rates in respect of some of the items; for example, some syrups, particularly rose syrup, and similar items are now levied GST at 18 per cent instead of earlier rates of 12 per cent. Also, GST rates of cosmetics and beauty products are fixed at 28 per cent since they are now classified as luxury items; many of these earlier used to attract much lower rates. According to a grocery shop owner interviewed, there is not much variation in the net profitability post GST. Except for cosmetics and beauty products, prices have remained practically unchanged for most items of common use by the consumers.

However, the grocery owner stated that while filing tax returns, he is facing hardship under the GST regime. No doubt the 22 GST Council meeting has given relief to businesses having annual turnover of less than ₹1.5 crore, now that they have to file returns once in a quarter, unlike in the first three months post GST when they had to submit monthly returns. That is good news. Still, under the GST regime, every grocery item has specific HSN Code carrying fixed GST rates. Filing returns matching the two for a large number of grocery items and all their variants is a highly tedious, time-taking and cumbersome process. Grocery shops generally place order with different vendors/distributors in bulk. When billing is done at the time of such bulk procurement from vendors, tax proceeds have to be calculated in accordance with respective HSN Codes and GST rates

---

[9] After the 23rd meeting of the GST Council on 10 November 2017, only 50 'sin' goods and luxury items now attract 28 per cent rate. Rates of most grocery items have been reduced from 28 per cent to 18 per cent and from 18 per cent to 12 per cent or 5 per cent, and for a few items, rate has been reduced from 5 per cent to nil.

identified for the specified items. The shop owner expressed his distress in terms of the practical difficulties—in time lost while matching items based on their HSN Codes and GST rates, etc. Since the procurement is generally done in bulk to facilitate consumers' demand, the billing and matching of invoices at the distributor–retailer level of the value chain is also quite tedious. The same is true at the retailer–consumer billing process. To avoid all these hassles and also to evade tax, many grocery stores are still using kaccha bills unhindered, the trader remarked. Further, since the GST software is getting updated from time to time, he finds that feeding item names based on respective HSN Codes is often difficult at the time of filing of returns. Moreover, when the GSTN is down, it is impossible to work on it on a time-bound manner. The government needs to take adequate steps to simplify the returns filing procedure, the shopkeeper added. Barring such complaints, the shop owner is cautiously optimistic about future prospects of GST.

Home Appliances

Going to home appliances business, our field investigation noticed positive attitudes among traders towards GST. In this sector, items are classified into three categories in general: small accessories, cookware and appliances. The GST rate for small accessories is 5 per cent; that for cookware is 12 per cent, while for appliances such as toaster, kettle and griller, the rate is 28 per cent. The government has kept appliances under the luxury items category attracting the maximum rate.[10] One trader interviewed said that the new system is more transparent for sure. But when it comes to convenience and business friendliness, he has serious reservations. The billing system keeps traders and buyers informed about the tax liabilities

---

[10] After the 23rd meeting of the GST Council on 10 November 2017, most home appliances are now taxed @ 18 per cent.

in respect of each item. The trader expressed satisfaction on the aspect of reimbursement of tax expenses under the GST regime. However, the home appliance trader was highly critical of monthly filing of returns envisaged under the GST regime, as his annual business turnover exceeded ₹1.5 crore. The procedure, according to him, is tedious, time-taking and extremely cumbersome. A huge amount of time and resources, approximately 7–10 days depending on the volume of business, are being spent on filing returns. This encroaches upon his time and affects normal business hours. According to the trader, the quarterly filing of returns under the older VAT system was much more convenient and manageable.

Another hassle with the GST system is that returns have to be filed very carefully. If there is a wrong figure entered and the returns are then being filed, then the wrong figure cannot be rectified/corrected. Under the VAT system, traders had the provision to correct wrong entries/figures even after filing the returns. But the GST software does not allow that. This has created extra hardship for traders while filing returns. At the same time, if there is a delay in filing returns, then the defaulters are liable to pay penalty on a daily basis, on top of the huge time spent every month in the process of filing returns. Many traders have insufficient computer literacy and education about the use of the GST software, and there has hardly been any attempt on the part of the government to train them on the software before launching GST and even thereafter. The webinars and awareness demonstrations conducted through public media so far seem to have been inadequate or have not reached all traders. During field investigation, the concerned trader indicated that while the government has implemented GST, proper steps have not being taken for its smooth implementation. Unless remedial measures are taken by the government in making the GST software hassle-free for traders, they will continue to face difficulties at the time of filing returns, the trader commented.

Automobile Parts and Service Sector

Turning over to the automobile sector, an internationally reputed leading brand's authorised service centre was visited as part of the fieldwork. Here, the response obtained was mixed. In the previous system, there used to be different excise duties and other state-level taxes in the procurement of automobile parts. That had a cascading effect on the prices for the customers and difficulty in estimation of final taxes for the company. Also, earlier the VAT on automobile parts was charged at 12.5 per cent. For example, if the automobile parts earlier cost say ₹1,000, then ₹875 was on actual price of parts, while ₹125 was on VAT. At the same time, variable excise duties and other state taxes had their own effects on the overall cost of automobile services. But now under GST, all excise duties and other state taxes have been eliminated. The new GST rate for automobile parts is fixed at 28 per cent. The GST rate for labour charges is now fixed at 18 per cent in place of earlier 15 per cent. Thus, if the parts are still to cost ₹1,000, then the price is to be reduced to ₹781.25 and GST would be ₹218.75.

In the first quarter after the roll-out of GST, the service provider had attempted to keep the prices of automobile parts the same by adjusting the prices of parts while keeping in mind GST rates. This might be a well-thought-through business move by this service provider to avoid any substantial business loss in the aftermath of GST. The company officials informed us that with the elimination of excise and state taxes after GST roll-out, the listed price at which automobile parts are now available has come down, and it has enabled service provider in many cases to keep the service cost for end-consumers unchanged. The reaction of consumers to VAT vis-à-vis GST-related differences does not yet show any distinctive preference for the current or the earlier regime.

With regard to labour charges, the service tax on labour charges under the earlier VAT regime was 15 per cent; Swachh

Bharat and Krishi Kalyan Cess were also imposed at 0.2 per cent each. There has been a marginal increase in the GST rate to 18 per cent now. The company officials interviewed said that such nominal hike on labour service has not significantly affected the volume of automobile service business so far. Hence, this is not a problem for them at this point of time. Here, one positive development is worth mentioning. In the earlier regime under VAT, there used to be proliferation of unauthorised automobile repair and washing shops that used to provide these services at much cheaper rate than authorised service centres. Such shops issued kaccha bills to customers and that way evaded tax. Customers also ended up paying less for such services, regard-less of the quality of service. To a large extent, that was a win-win outcome for such traders and customers. Now, according to the official, the GST regime has definitely been successful in curtailing such businesses practised by many roadside service vendors, but precisely why he could not tell, while expressing the confidence that GST has the promise of streamlining the entire automobile service and repair business.

That being said, one area of concern expressed by com-pany official interviewed is regarding monthly filing of returns, which has become more tedious. There has been a quantum jump in the paper work in the form of collating all the bills and entering them online. Now that GST rates have been fixed for all kinds of automobile parts and ancillary services like labour, the entire procedure of filing returns has become too cumber-some. If the government can make the return filing system sim-pler and hassle-free, then much of the problem related to GST will get resolved automatically.

Mobile Phones

While exploring mobile phone and smartphone segment, an interesting scenario has emerged. An official of a highly reputed mobile phone store in Delhi/NCR said that earlier during the

VAT era, there were two different tax rates on mobile phones. Any set above ₹10,000 used to attract VAT at 12.5 per cent, while a mobile phone set below ₹10,000 used to attract VAT at 5 per cent. Under the current GST regime, there is a single tax rate at 12 per cent (CGST at 6% and SGST at 6%) for all mobile phone and smartphone models irrespective of their price range. Because of slightly reduced tax rates for premier segment smartphones, their prices have also declined marginally. However, for basic models of smartphones, the company generally determines a lower price so that after adjusting for GST, there is not much change in the sale price. This measure is aimed at retaining the customer base post GST. For accessories, there is a hike in sale price post GST. For accessories such as phone covers, considered a luxury product under GST, the tax rate is fixed at 28 per cent vis-à-vis 5 per cent under the VAT era.

While purchasing mobile phones and smartphones, end-consumers always prefer finance schemes using EMI (equated monthly instalment). Under GST, there is a catch in the finance scheme vis-à-vis under the earlier VAT regime. Now there is an additional GST component imposed in EMI unlike earlier. This has hiked up the EMIs ranging between minimum ₹80 and 100, and sometimes even higher due to the interest component which was often waived during the earlier regime. Hence post GST, this has caused reduction in the sale of smartphones via finance mechanism that used to be the catalyst for their bumper sale under VAT. The mobile phone trader commented that this was true for other forms of EMI schemes across the board. While traders want that banks should stop GST imposition on EMIs, banks are not willing to compromise. In this situation, the government needs to intervene to settle the issue, the trader added. Additionally, problems related to monthly filing of returns exist in this sector too. Now it is more expensive for the company to hire chartered accountants on a monthly basis to file returns. Thus, the scenario as unfolding in the post-GST era reflects a mixed trend.

Optical Products

The situation was also assessed among small traders in other sectors such as optical and pharmaceutical outlets. The optical shop owner was not much excited about his business prospects in the short term in the aftermath of GST. According to him, the market is down in the first place because of higher GST rates on optical products as compared to the rates that prevailed earlier. Currently, there are three slabs under GST for optical items—12 per cent on contact lenses and similar items and 18 per cent on spectacles (normal glasses) as compared to 5.25 per cent for contact lenses and spectacles, and 12.5 per cent for sunglasses, which are considered as luxury products under the new tax regime.[11] Increase in tax rates under GST has led to a general hike in prices of optical items. During the festival season, the impact of price rise was negative, and the prospect did not look very positive for small traders in this sector in the short term, while there is an air of cautious optimism in respect of the long-term benefits.

The shop owner is unhappy about the fact that post GST, importers/distributors of optical products are not passing on the benefits of GST input tax reimbursement down the value chain to retailers and end consumers. Hence, the price of the same spectacle remains artificially high at retail shops for final sale to end-consumers. According to the retailer, the government must act quickly to ensure that the reimbursement benefits reach retailers and end-consumers. Retailers in general are now forced to buy products at high prices from distributors and sell at high prices to end-consumers, which ideally should be reversed under GST. According to him, the GST system has to be

---

[11] After the 23rd meeting of the GST Council on 10 November 2017, GST on intraocular lens and on frames and mountings for spectacles, goggles or the like, and parts thereof has been reduced from 18% to 12%. That on goggles has been reduced from 28% to 18%.

implemented more effectively by the government so that every-body complies with the new system. In the present moment, some are taking advantage of GST reimbursements while others down the value chain are deprived of such benefits.

Pharmacy (Medical) Stores

Turning to the pharmaceutical sector, we made field visits to two pharmacy outlets—one is a chain of an established brand and the other a local medical store. The established brand pharmacy outlet official said that after the roll-out of GST, there have been some fluctuations in the retail prices so far. Different medicines have different GST rates which attract different rates of 12 per cent, 5 per cent and even no sales tax or 0 per cent rate. GST rate for most medicines now is 12 per cent instead of 9.5 per cent earlier that included VAT and excise duty. These medicines have thus witnessed an increase in MRP. GST rate for some other medicines such as ORS, insulin and vaccines is 5 per cent, same as the earlier VAT rate. So there is no change in the MRP of such medicines. The established brand pharmacy outlet representative further indicated that MRP for some commonly used essential medicines related to blood pressure, diabetes and fever (i.e., Paracetamol, etc.) have been reduced from the branded health care company side. In such cases, the customers are getting relief. But the health care company has also marginally increased the MRP at their own end on some other medicines that are not daily usable ones. In the end, he gives an impression that such a move has taken the interest of both customers and company and that with the roll-out of GST, there has not been much change in their business volume, while customers are also generally happy and receiving pucca bills.

In contrast, the local medical shop owner was quite unhappy on GST. He is of the opinion that the GST regime has, by and large, increased the MRP of most of the medicines, including common medicines that are used on a daily basis, which has adversely affected their business. Even the prices of tinned baby food items have also increased by minimum ₹65 to ₹85 depending on the size of the container. When asked about filing of tax returns, the shop owner commented that with the relaxation made in the 22nd GST Council meeting, they need to do it quarterly, which will bring some welcome relief.

Electronics and Electrical Products

Turning into the arena of electronics and electrical products, some new developments were observed during the course of field investigation. The GST regime has designated such items in the category of luxury products. Under the previous system, electronic products such as geysers, electric irons, heaters, fans and toasters were levied at VAT + surcharge = 12.5 per cent + 5 per cent on 12.5 = 13.25 per cent in total. To this, excise duty was also added at 12.5 per cent. Thus, the overall tax component on electronics was around 26 per cent. Under the GST regime, single tax slab at 28 per cent has been fixed on electronics products.[12] This is actually a marginal increase in the tax component. Consequently, there has not been any significant increase in the prices at which it is distributed to the retailers and finally sold to end-consumers. However, at times customers are not willing to pay higher price due to enhanced tax rate even if the hike in tax rate is marginal, the trader remarked. In that case, they postpone their purchase decisions. This has slowed down business at least temporarily, or in the short run. But the trader is hopeful that things will pick up in this segment of business in the near future and GST will ultimately be beneficial.

---

[12] After the 23rd meeting of the GST Council, these now mostly attract 18 per cent rate like the electrical cables and wires discussed hereafter.

Cable Wire Connection: Industrial and Commercial Projects

The other side of the electrical product market deals with industrial and commercial business for building infrastructure, for example, construction of multi-storey apartments by real estate builders, construction of shopping complexes and electric connection to turnkey projects. These are critical areas of electrical business and might lead to diversification into several newer projects. The trader who was interviewed said that most of his business relates to this category. As a retailer, he provides big-size cable wires wounded in huge wheel type of frame to infrastructure and turnkey projects. Under VAT, the tax rate in such electrical business was fixed at 13.25 per cent. The roll-out of GST has increased the tax rate from 13.25 per cent to 28 per cent. This is a more than 15 per cent hike, which is quite significant.

The rise in prices has in turn resulted in a substantial shrinkage of the profit margin post GST, sometimes by almost 50 per cent, as per his estimates, from about 10–12 per cent earlier to only 5–6 per cent now. The cumulative effect of such a drastic fall in profit margin, especially in respect of bulk industrial business dealing with electrical cable wires, is causing unhappiness to all traders in this sector. At the same time, traders like this are surprised that the government has kept cable wire among luxury items under the GST regime. To them, cable wire is an essential item in the electrical goods market and is used quite significantly in industrial/infrastructural turnkey projects. Hence, the government should reconsider and take cable wire out from the category of luxury items, he added.

LED Lights: Electrical Products

The silver lining in the electrical goods market is that the tax rate for LED lights has been reduced to 12 per cent under the GST regime in comparison to 18 per cent under VAT. This is a smart move on the part of the government towards incentivising the use of LED bulbs that reduce power consumption. Reduction in the GST rate on LED items is expected to reduce their price and increase business volume, one trader in this sector apprised us during the market survey. On the issue of filing returns, he says that because his annual turnover exceeds ₹1.5 crore, he requires monthly filing of returns, which is a difficult process to undergo and is not convenient. At the same time, it is financially burdensome since accountants hired need to be paid professional fees on a monthly basis, the trader remarked.

On the whole, the impression obtained from dealers in electronics and electrical products has been a mixed bag again. However, the traders in general seem to be optimistic on the issue of GST prospects in the long term, while they want the government to address the short-term hitches quickly.

Stationery Items

While interviewing a shop owner of a stationery items store, we found that most of the stationery items such as notebooks, pencils, pens and files of different sizes and shapes attract 12 per cent GST rate. The trader did not find any perceptible change in business volume or margin post GST. Because such stationery items are generally not expensive, the impact of GST on their prices is not that much alarming too, the shop owner says. Regarding colour printing, colour photocopy, etc. as part of stationery items, now with GST rate having been reduced to 12 per cent from earlier 18 per cent, it has brought considerable relief to consumers. He says that until the old stocks of stationery items are not sold out, there will be temporary loss in profitability in respect of these items since MRP of such items was lower. However, he is confident that once the new stock with revised MRP comes in, things will definitely improve. The good news is that most of the problems faced by small traders of such stationery items have now been addressed by the 22nd GST Council meeting. Also, relaxation in filing of returns by making it on a quarterly basis was welcomed by the shop owner interviewed.

Courier Business

In the courier industry, there has not been much impact on the profitability or business volume under the new GST regime. While interacting with a representative of an internationally reputed courier company operating in India, we were given to understand that there were some technical glitches in operational and logistical aspects of the business as a consequence of GST, leading to slowing down of the delivery process, with concomitant delay in the recovery of payment from vendors and customers (particularly corporate customers). This is because until the time the recipients actually got themselves registered with the GSTN with valid GSTINs, they were not able to generate pucca bill for the shipment to get delivered at the point of destination. Hence, on such technical delays, revenue collection and delivery of consignments got impacted adversely. However, that was not the case with individual customers having or not having GSTIN. However, they expect these problems to be temporary and to be resolved soon.

International Logistics

On similar lines, an international logistics company official says that earlier under the VAT regime, many dishonest manufacturers/traders used to evade paying excise duties at the time of importing inputs for the purpose of manufacturing of goods for re-export purposes. Such traders used to take advantages of the lack of a foolproof system of tax payments. Again while re-exporting their finished products by using the services of international logistics companies, such defaulting manufacturers used to claim duty drawback. That way, many of the unscrupulous manufacturers/traders not only evaded taxes that they had an obligation to pay to the government but also took benefits of duty drawback from the government. With the roll-out of GST, such malpractices have been brought under control. Under GST, the duty drawback would only be available for the customs duty paid on imported inputs. Also, now all transactions prior to export have to be listed and invoices of buyers and sellers matched to claim input tax credit. In the case of any accounting discrepancy, the default-ing traders' goods will be detected, held up and penalties/ fines slapped. Thus, GST has enabled bringing many traders/ manufacturers under the tax network. The system has become more foolproof to eliminate leakages and tax evasion in the export trade business.

In the case of inter-state transaction of inputs, an exporter is required to file a shipping bill for the goods. The shipping bill will be considered as an application for refund of IGST paid in inter-state transactions solely for the purpose of export. Input tax credit will be provided as a refund under GST instead of previously applicable duty drawback schemes. The systematic computerised system under the GST regime has also enabled international logistics companies to be more vig-ilant on export shipment. The government is sending notifica-tions from time to time to such logistics firms on ways to deal with export shipments in accordance with the provisions of GST regulations. The official of the international logistics firm interviewed is of the opinion that implementation of GST is a step in the right direction. It will further regularise export business in the long term.

Tipping Issues: Raising Awareness

The general impression gathered after the market survey is a picture that is still evolving in which hope and caution, opti-mism and fear are mixed together and no clear picture really emerges. But still we could sense an overall air of satisfaction among the majority of the respondents about the simplicity, elimination of cascading effect, ease of transaction (barring the return filing and reimbursement of input tax credit) and transparency that GST has brought and the hope shared by the majority that things will get better in future and GST will make all stakeholders better off. Seamless transition to a software-driven system is proving to be difficult no doubt, and the government needs to focus on training, mentoring and handholding in deserving cases. Traders and businesses seem to have understood and become reconciled to the reality that taxes are not evadable any longer and these have to be paid even if it increases their business costs. There is also increasing realisation that formalisation of the informal sector is a necessity for both to survive, even though it will put heavier burden on the informal sector in the beginning, but these pains are unavoidable. They only want some understanding and accommodation from the government so that the process of transition may not lead to the end of their businesses.

Another tipping issue related to GST is with regard to technological glitches. People at large are hopeful that such problems are temporary and will soon be resolved, yet the teething issues are causing them serious handicaps, and often leaving them drained of any working capital due to the delay in refunds of the input tax credit. For example, some business people have complained that the GSTN reacts very slowly to some data that have been already entered into the system. When a business enterprise files a return or pays the tax online, the GSTN accepts it but for a few days the website does not give confirmation on the receipt of such returns or payments. In such cases, the website still displays the status as pending. In such a situation, the trader/business enterprise cannot track the status of such entries, and the refunds get blocked. This absence of information about payment status creates anxiety in the minds of many traders, particularly if the amount of such payment is large. Further, many a time it takes considerably longer to get a GSTIN even after registering with the GSTN. In such situations, the transaction process in the value chain gets held up until the dealer gets the GSTIN. This leads to inconvenience in processing payment-related information, particularly for the purpose of claiming input tax credit wherever applicable. Such technological glitches need to be fixed as early as possible. These problems were shared by many of the respondents in the course of our market survey.

With regard to complaints from various segments of population, particularly traders and general people, the government has provided some relief after the 22nd GST Council meeting by further simplifying the rules and giving considerable relief to small businesses and exporters. GST rates on 27 products have also been slashed, which will bring relief to both the concerned dealers and end-consumers. In particular, reduction of GST rate on man-made yarn was a key demand of textile traders in states such as Gujarat and is bound to give relief to them.[13] All these steps adopted by the government indicate its responsiveness which was welcomed by all respondents universally.

Voice of the Consumers

Consumer interviews were conducted according to their profiles such as age, occupation, gender, education level and social status such as housewives, working ladies, working men, students and professionals as outlined in Table 6.2. Voices of the consumers were also equally revealing and insightful in assessing the impact of GST. Here, the response showed a clear swing in favour of GST in terms of its present and potential future benefits. Most consumers say that even if they might be facing

---

[13] *The Times of India*, 'Govt's GST relief measures: Highlights', *The Times of India*, 7 October 2017. Available at: https://timesofindia.indiatimes.com/ business/india-business/govts-gst-relief-measures-highlights/article-show/60974381.cms (accessed on 13 December 2017).

some temporary problem or some hike in their monthly budgets because of GST, they are still positive that the long-term implications of the reform would make them economically better off in future. Majority of consumers interviewed, barring very few, support the government on GST and are ready to accept the claims of the government that GST will curb tax evasion and black money and will make India a common efficient market to the advantage of all stakeholders. General response of consumers is summarised in Table 6.3.

Tax Administrator's Perspectives

A very significant part of our empirical study concerned a candid and insightful interview with a senior tax administrator, without which this study would have remained incomplete. He considers GST a very remarkable economic policy intervention of the government. We outline his perspectives in Table 6.4.

Summing Up

During the span of the last four months since the landmark tax reform was launched, GST has been at the centre stage of all debates and discussions dominating public space. Whether it is political parleys, academic circles, industry forums, print and electronic media, social media and even in living room conversations at homes, it has been the most intriguing, contentious and engaging topic of discussion. People from all walks of life are impacted by GST, but the impact will become more overwhelming as it slowly stabilises. Once stabilised, GST will impact each one of us in many ways, and it has the potential to transform our national economy. Our economic growth, national financial management, consumers' domestic budgets and investment plans, and their spending behaviour will all be determined or strongly influenced by GST, and lot more debates

Table 6.3: Summary of Consumers' Responses

Category of Consumers	Response
Working Ladies–Housewives	Opinions are divided regarding the impact of GST on monthly budgets, with a slender majority asserting that there has been no significant change. Most support GST for its long-term benefits. Rest of housewives/working ladies are of the opinion that GST has increased their budget by 5–10 per cent, especially on grocery items. In particular prices of packed food such as pulses, gram flour and flour, thread, and small packets of hair dyes have increased under GST. This contradicts what we have found earlier from the traders. Housewives say that LPG cylinders have become more expensive after GST rate of 5 per cent imposed on them. Earlier, its price was ₹630 and now it is ₹653. Eating food in restaurants and using salon services have become more expensive. Restaurant owners are not reducing price on food served. This contradicts what the restaurants say, as detailed earlier.
Working Men	There is no discernible change so far in the daily/monthly budgets. By and large, they are supportive of GST. One consumer is unhappy that kaccha bill businesses are still rampant on products such as curtains and similar items. Such traders are giving a Hobson's choice to the consumers: If they want kaccha bill, they would not charge GST and accept cash for the goods sold. If consumers want pucca bill, then they would charge GST. There is no check on this, and consumer behaviour is predictable in this scenario.
Undergraduate Students–Young Generation	Their reaction has been mixed. They are unable to assess future benefits prematurely and unwilling to pass judgement on them. Their monthly budgets have increased in the range of ₹1,000–1,500.
Lady School Teacher	Monthly budget on groceries has increased marginally. Buying electronics products like television has become more expensive with 28 per cent GST rate now being imposed. EMI charges of banks have gone up substantially with additional documentation required by them.

(Continued)

Table 6.3: *(Continued)*

Category of Consumers	Response
Postgraduate Consumers	The reactions in general are evenly split between support and criticism for GST. Perhaps it is too early to make an assessment. Some took objection to the fact that online trading through e-commerce portals has become more expensive.
Young/Middle-aged Working Executives	According to one consumer, there is not much perceptible change in the monthly budget. He is highly supportive of GST and asserts that this should have been implemented a long time ago. Another consumer says lunches and dinners at restaurants are more expensive now, which is causing inconvenience. But generally they are supportive of GST and are hopeful about its future benefits.
Retired Senior Executive in Private Sector	There is no perceptible change in their daily/monthly budgets in general. He is highly supportive of GST and says that such a move should have been initiated long time ago. He strongly believes that GST will be beneficial in future.
Accounting Professional as Consumer	The new regime may be good for economy, but the implementation or execution is not up to mark. Kirana traders are not passing on benefits of input tax credits on end-consumers. They are taking advantage of consumers' ignorance. Grocery stores are charging higher price for milk and dairy products as well in the pretext of GST even when there is 0 per cent GST rate on such items. Fresh vegetable vendors have inflated the price of products saying there is no supply from distributors/*mandi*, despite the fact that GST rate is 0 per cent on fresh vegetables. Vegetable vendors have raised prices on such items. The government should take action on such unscrupulous traders, he added.
Retired Army Personnel Currently Working in Private Sector	There is only some marginal increase in the monthly budget. Those having agricultural land complained that post GST, all agriculture-related items such as manure, high-yielding seeds and fertilisers have become more expensive for farmers. Earlier such products used to be traded in cash and were cheaper. Now with GST, they have become more expensive, causing inconvenience to farmers. But despite this, he expresses full support for GST, saying the government has done the right thing by implementing GST.

Table 6.4: Views of Tax Administrator

Issues Raised	Comments
How is GST going to impact common man's life?	Unlike VAT, cascading effects of the embedded taxes are now eliminated under the GST regime. Hence, price level in the market is going to fall in general. That benefits common man's budget conditions. Over a period of time with heightened competition in the market post GST, prices will further stabilise. On the issue of traders not passing on input tax credit benefits to the end-consumers, he says that government needs to take strict action on this to reverse the trend. Anti-profiteering clause,[a] when introduced, will further enforce compliance on such matters. However, the government is in favour of using it sparingly to begin with.
Will GST lead to freedom from tax terrorism/ inspector raj?	With the GSTN being fully operational, tax administration is now fully automated. Self-policing mechanism is robust to detect any tax fraud, with all registrations and transactions being done online under GST and filing and processing of all transactions also being online. Too many verifications and seeking permissions from lower-level tax officials are no longer needed by honest taxpayers. Incidents of sudden raids, retrospective changes of tax provisions and reopening of old returns will also be greatly reduced and eliminated. Tax officials under the GST regime can no longer extort money from taxpayers. Cumulative effects of all these safeguards under the GST regime will collectively ensure elimination of tax terrorism/inspector raj.
Will GST be able to curb black money and corruption?	Self-policing mechanism and automated system enabled by the GSTN together ensure mandatory matching of invoices between buyers and sellers in the value chain. Consequently, tendency of people to sell without invoice will greatly diminish. Cash transactions will be minimised and tax evasion will be checked effectively. Once reverse charge mechanism is implemented, possibilities of tax evasion will be further reduced.[b] All these factors together will greatly reduce generation of black money under the GST regime. Additionally, the central government is soon going to implement e-way system (electronic wavering system).[c] That will do away with all check posts for inter-state movement of goods. These were the main causes of corruption under VAT.

(Continued)

Table 6.4: (Continued)

Issues Raised	Comments
	Cumulative effect of all these safety measures collectively will lead to curbing black money and corruption.
How is GST going to ease the burden of filing multiple tax returns vis-à-vis VAT?	Earlier under VAT, returns were to be filed quarterly, while tax payments were being made on a monthly basis. Under the earlier excise duties, both returns and tax payments had to be done monthly, and under the service tax, returns had to be filed half yearly while tax payments were made on monthly basis. Under the present GST regime, traders with yearly turnover of less than ₹1.5 crore have to file returns on a quarterly basis. Others with annual turnovers above ₹1.5 crore have to do it on a monthly basis. Multiple tax rates are now eliminated, and online filing of returns has made tax administration simple. Overall, the new system will be helpful in easing the burden on traders, once the GST software settles down and the pending technology-related glitches are all eliminated.
Will GST be able to make consumers the king?	Under the GST regime, consumers will have a lot of choices on their purchase decisions. GST will be very effective in enhancing healthy competition in the market on a level playing field. It will ensure that best market practices prevail in the market on a long-term basis and promote greater transparency and accountability in the market. All these are positive forces under the GST regime working collectively to empower consumers and make them the real king of the marketplaces all over India.

Notes: [a]Please see Chapter 5 for details on the anti-profiteering clause.

[b]Reverse charge mechanism has been discussed in Chapter 4.

[c]Under e-way bill system, all traders/consigners dispatching goods with value exceeding ₹50,000 have to obtain an e-way bill through the GSTN. The bill will contain details of the goods and mention the states through which the consignment will be transported. All such details will also be available on the mobile phones of the tax officials in the concerned states. When the truck/transport will cross the border between such states, they will not have to wait in long lines of check posts and offer bribes, which were regularly happening under the earlier VAT regime. Under the GST regime, only a handful of consignments will be scrutinised randomly, using a technology-driven risk assessment mechanism. Hence, the e-way bill system to be implemented soon under GST will eliminate the possibilities of black money and corruption. This is going to be a tremendous benefit of the new GST regime.

and arguments should take place on such an all-encompassing and revolutionary reform to keep it on the right track.

Now the question is: To what extent GST has been able to make a positive impact among various stakeholders? Or has it been able to win over the heart and mind of majority of stakeholders? What percentage of population is unhappy with the new system? Our survey only provides a cursory glimpse into such issues without being able to cast any great illumination on these questions; the time for such assessments has not come yet. But these are very important questions that need to be addressed by all concerned parties—government, business and general public. Problems are bound to be there for sure when we have unleashed a disruptive reform of such magnitude. But how soon such problems can be resolved will test the government's resolve as well as the limits to people's endurance. As ascertained from a small segment of the market, people by and large are still optimistic about the potential of GST for making the lot better for majority of stakeholders; it has given people a sense of empowerment and the freedom from inspector raj. While these positive sentiments are clearly discernible in the market, challenges are no less staggering. A proactive and participatory approach on the part of the government to fix the problems is the need of the hour. The decisions made during the 22nd GST Council meeting have sent the right signals and given an impression to the key stakeholders that GST will be steered in a manner that is going to be beneficial for all in the long run. The government should not fall short of making such bold decisions in future too as and when required.

The overall impression obtained from our field survey and interaction with various stakeholders—traders/business groups, consumers and tax administrators—has been generally positive when it comes to the long-term benefits. However, the short-term challenges are not only real but also serious, and the government has to be responsive and proactive to fulfil the expectations of the people. That alone will win the hearts and minds of the people of India and garner all-round support for the new tax regime, creating an enabling environment in turn for launching further transformational reforms like this one and weave the fabric of our socio-economic life for an all-inclusive development of the nation.

In the course of our long journey through this book, we have derived an abiding faith that GST has a great future for our country and that We, the People of India, will be the ultimate beneficiary of this bold and landmark reform. It will give us greater freedom of choices, promote healthy competition in the market, institute global best practices in our system and establish much higher levels of transparency and accountability in all spheres of our national life. We have strong conviction that GST will ultimately empower the consumers and make them the true kings of the market, and we end this book with this unwavering faith in our hearts.

Index

About the Authors

Govind Bhattacharjee is a civil service officer currently working as Director General at the office of the Comptroller and Auditor General (CAG) of India in New Delhi. During his more than three-decade-long service career, he has held many important positions in India and abroad. Bhattacharjee is a prolific writer on a wide variety of subjects ranging from physics to economics. He is a regular contributor to national newspapers and academic journals on current socio-economic and developmental issues. He has earlier published books on public finance and popular science, besides authoring a seminal work on the 11 special category states of India (*Special Category States of India*, 2016). His other areas of interest include public policy, developmental economics, international relations and federalism.

Debasis Bhattacharya is an academician and currently a senior faculty member at Amity Business School, Amity University, Gurgaon. He is a member of the Centre for BRICS Studies, a Centre of Excellence in the university. Bhattacharya received his doctorate in political science from the University of Oregon, USA. He received his MA in international studies from the Josef Korbel School of International Studies, University of Denver, USA, and MA in economics from Delhi School of Economics, University of Delhi, India. He has 18 years of teaching and research experience in India and the USA. His interest areas include international political economy, international relations, international trade policy, international business, international diplomacy and international organisations.